GRILL TO PERFECTION

TWO CHAMPION PIT MASTERS SHARE RECIPES AND TECHNIQUES FOR UNFORGETTABLE BACKYARD GRILLING

PHOTOGRAPHY BY KEN GOODMAN

ANDY HUSBANDS AND CHRIS HART
WINNERS OF THE JACK DANIEL'S WORLD CHAMPIONSHIP INVITATIONAL BARBECUE CONTEST
AND ANDREA PYENSON

PAGE STREET
PUBLISHING CO.

CONTENTS

FOREWORD

I met Andy Husbands over a mouthful of smoked pork butt. It was mutual admiration at first bite. Andy is a rarity among chefs—a guy who not only runs an edgy restaurant in Boston's Back Bay, but can slow-smoke with the best of them on the competition barbecue circuit. He certainly has the trophies—Jack Daniel's World Championship Invitational Barbecue Grand Champions, American Royal Barbecue Competition 1st Place Brisket, with his team, iQUE Barbecue—to prove it.

Not only that, but the guy can write. In prose so evocative you can smell the wood smoke and taste the chili hellfire. In recipes so clear and concise, they're like watching Andy over his shoulder while he cooks.

Having written extensively about the art of smoking (in *Wicked Good Barbecue*) and everything you need to know about building the ultimate burger (*Wicked Good Burgers*), Andy and iQUE teammate Chris Hart now turn their attention to a topic near and dear to my heart: grilling. The first thing you'll be pleased to know is that everyone is welcomed under their tent: gas grillers, charcoal grillers, partisans of kettle grills, hibachis, komodo cookers and more.

The second thing is that Andy and Chris approach what is all too often a technique clouded with dogma and superstition with the logic and discipline of scientists, laying out clear descriptions of direct grilling, two-zone grilling, high- and low-heat grilling and smoke-grilling.

But they're hardly stern theoreticians, no. A passion for big flavors and a generous dose of whimsy infuse every page. Their recipes are ecumenical enough to include Thai-Flavored Pork Belly Skewers, Slow Grilled Alabama Chicken Thighs with Alabama White Sauce, Grilled Narragansett Pizza, Tofu Tacos and Elvis' Grilled Banana Split.

If you're a beginner, *Grill to Perfection* will teach you a lot, and if you're an experienced griller already, the book will help you take your skills to the next level. Either way, you'll eat awesome food and have a lot of fun grilling it.

Steven Raichlen

INTRODUCTION

Grilling to us is more than a way to cook. It's a way of life, a form of expression steeped in history and tradition. We clearly remember growing up in the mean streets of Needham, Massachusetts, with the smell of lighter fluid wafting through the air on a hot summer day. Hot dogs and hamburgers and great times with friends and families were sure to follow. All of us have grown up with similar memories and continue to create them in our lives today.

Historically, grilling is as old as civilization, or at least as old as fire—some 500,000 years. By now it is deeply rooted in cuisines throughout the world. In the United States, backyard grilling became popular after World War I, when families began moving to the suburbs. Today, grilling at home is moving way beyond the charred steaks, hot dogs and hamburgers of the 1950s. (If you're looking to see how far burgers have come, see our last book, *Wicked Good Burgers*; it will rock your burger world.)

Grill to Perfection is about grilling, and for us, as in all of our books, technique is the key. Because temperatures can vary pretty dramatically in a grill, it's important to develop a feel for the fire, rather than rigidly follow recipes. Once you master the temperatures and timing on a grill, the sky's the limit. Read the following, learn it, practice it, love it and become grill masters like us.

GRILLS

Basically, there are two types of grills: charcoal (which includes wood burning) and gas. Both have their merits, and all of the recipes in this book work on gas and charcoal grills.

The heat coming from gas grills is measured in BTUs (British Thermal Units) and we think, to be effective, a grill has to have more than 100 BTUs per square inch. Refer to the manual that comes with your grill to get the optimum heat. For a lot of the recipes in this book, we want a super hot grill, and this is an important measurement to achieve that. With a higher BTU output, you will use more gas; trust us—this is worth it. We've seen too many of those small tailgating grills that are basically food warmers. They do little more than cook your food through, adding nothing to the flavor. For many—though not all—recipes, you need that heat.

We get it. We know why you bought and love your gas grill. It lights quickly and is easier to clean. We're not averse to using one, but when we have a choice, we'll use our charcoal grills. Charcoal grills are available in three categories: kettle, flat and ceramic.

➔ Kettle grills are by far the most well known and widely used. Shaped like globes, with coal sitting on the bottom and a grill grate above, they have vents on the top of the lid and on the bottom. The Weber 22-inch/56cm kettle grill is the gold standard.

→ Flat grills are rectangular, with flat bottoms, and can be much shallower than kettles. They can be small like hibachis or large like half of a giant oil drum. The coal sits on the bottom and there are air vents on all sides.

→ Ceramic grills are heavy and not very mobile. If you buy one of these, it will live in your yard. But we love them because they can get extremely hot, retain heat and hold consistent temperatures beautifully—once you master cooking in them. They have vents on the top and bottom. Word of caution: they tend to be on the expensive side.

All of these are fantastic options and burn at a higher temperature than gas. This is the key to getting a char that we all love so much. There is a little more cleaning involved and it takes a little longer to light than gas, but we think the sear and smoky flavor make up for the extra effort.

NOT ALL CHARCOAL IS CREATED EQUAL

There are basically two types of charcoal: hardwood lump and briquettes. Both have their advantages, though when push comes to shove we are definitely hardwood lump guys.

Most of us grew up on charcoal briquettes, which are still used by 94 percent of backyard grillers. They are harder to light, easy to find and burn at a consistent temperature that is lower than hardwood, which is nice when you are slow-roasting. One problem with briquettes is that manufacturers use chemicals to bind them; some are even soaked in accelerants to make them light even faster. We would absolutely stay away from the latter because we feel the taste of whatever they are soaked in leaches into the food. If you want to use briquettes, we suggest seeking out natural briquettes, which are bound with vegetable starch and provide a cleaner flavor.

A lot of people also use lighter fluid with briquettes. We recommend a charcoal chimney instead because, like the chemicals used to bind some briquettes, lighter fluid can leach into food, adversely affecting the flavor. In our opinion, lighter fluid doesn't save you any time, either.

Andy fell in love with hardwood lump charcoal at East Coast Grill in Cambridge, Massachusetts, where he honed his live-fire cooking skills. These coals burn hotter than briquettes. This is perfect for the essence of grilling, which is about speed and sear. It is important to note that lump charcoal from different manufacturers burns differently. As with everything, some brands are better than others. By experimenting with different ones, you will learn their profiles and determine which you like best. (See our sidebar on charcoal selection [page 153] and the Resources section [page 184] for some of our favorites.)

HE TOOLS WE ALWAYS HAVE WHEN WE GRILL

Thermapen or stick thermometer: This is a pocket-size, instant-read thermometer that provides the temperature of food immediately.

Probe thermometer: This device allows you to monitor the temperature of the food and the air in the grill without opening the cover.

Multiple long metal, spring-release tongs, both 12 inches/30.5cm and 18 inches/45.7cm: We recommend always flipping meat with tongs, rather than using a fork, which pierces the meat, causing juice to escape. We like to have a variety on hand. The longer ones work well for adding charcoal to the fire; shorter ones are perfect for flipping food.

Offset metal spatula: This small, thin spatula is helpful for lifting and turning delicate food on the grill. The handle is angled slightly higher and away from the blade, which makes it easier to slide it under the food.

Fish spatula: This thin, spare metal spatula is extremely flexible and lightweight, with an upright front edge that allows you to lift and loosen foods from an angle; it's perfect for turning fish on a grill.

Side towels: The grilling area should be as clean as possible; spills can lead to flare-ups. Always have several cotton towels on hand to wipe up spills before they create problems. When folded, they also work as pot holders, and you can wipe your hands on them.

Charcoal chimney starter: We always use a chimney to start our fires. Fill it with coals, then light newspaper to start the fire. You'll never have to use lighter fluid again.

Heatproof/grilling gloves: This is essential, both for moving food around on the grate and for transferring lit charcoal from the chimney to the grill; oven mitts protect you from heat but won't give you the same dexterity as gloves.

Cast-iron pans: A lot of our recipes call for setting fire-resistant pans over the fire; cast iron is the best material for maintaining heat, the skillets last forever and they develop a nonstick surface as they age.

Fire extinguisher: See Safety First, on the following page, flare-ups are bound to happen.

Grill brush: Burnt food bits from your last grilling session definitely won't enhance your current one, so have a strong grill brush on hand to scrape them away before every new session.

Vegetable oil for grill cleaning: Oiling the grill after you scrape away leftovers helps keep food from sticking (but nothing will prevent it entirely).

Cans of craft beer: If we have to explain this, you may need more help than we can provide. Root beer is

Generally, people don't use logs in home grills, but a lot of home cooks use lump hardwood or fruitwood chips to add flavor to what they are cooking. The chips may not be worth it in fast-cooking items like burgers, but in longer process foods, like slow-grilled turkey or baby back ribs, it can take the flavor from great to superb.

SAFETY FIRST

When you are grilling, no matter which type of fuel you use, always have a fire extinguisher and water nearby. Even the pros do this. Fire is your friend but can easily turn into a frenemy.

LIGHTING AND CLEANING THE GRILL

If you are using a gas grill, just turn the gas on, first from the tank, then the unit. Push the igniter to make sure it lights everywhere. You should be able to see the fire under the grates and feel the heat by holding your hand a few inches above the grates. When you're done, always turn off the gas at the tank. Safety first.

For charcoal, we recommend starting the fire with a charcoal chimney (see Tools). Begin by preparing the grill. For direct grilling, spread an even bed across the bottom of the grill. For two-zone grilling, pile the unlit charcoal along one side of the grill. (We'll expand on these methods in a minute.) Then fill the chimney with coal, crumple newspaper, stuff it below the coals and light the newspaper. For a low fire, fill the chimney one-third full; for a medium fire, fill it half full; for a hot fire, fill it all the way. Wait about 10 minutes for the charcoal to become fully ignited. Flames should be just starting to peek through the top of the pile and you should not be able to hold your hand over it for more than a second (yeah, that hot). Carefully, wearing heatproof gloves, pour the lit charcoal evenly over the unlit charcoal in the grill.

Nobody says, "I can't wait to clean my grill." We know this. But we approach the chore by looking at why we do it, and that makes it a lot more enjoyable. Without a clean grill you could end up with food chunks from the last time you cooked (gross, no matter how good that food was), your food will stick and/or tear, and you could experience flare-ups or an outright fire—and then you're going out for dinner.

The key to cleaning your grill is getting it really hot first, so the best time to clean it is right after lighting it. When the grate is hot, it's time to clean. Give the grate a good brushing with a hard wire grill brush. We like to spray the grill grate with cooking oil spray or lightly dip a clean towel in a little bit of vegetable oil and rub the grates. Brush the grates again, then rub again. Repeat this process until the grates are clean of all debris. They don't need to look brand new, just clean. A little seasoning on the grate is okay.

COOKING METHODS

There are two basic grilling techniques: direct and two-zone. Each yields a distinctly different result and we highly recommend mastering and using both. For example, you don't want to slow roast or bake over direct heat because you run a pretty high risk of burning the food. Conversely, you'll never get a sear or char if you aren't working directly over the fire. If you want to look at it another way, direct heat is comparable to sautéing. Cooking with indirect heat, in a covered grill, is similar to roasting or baking.

DIRECT GRILLING

Direct grilling is all about speed. Unlike barbecue (see our first book, *Wicked Good Barbecue*), which is cooked slow and low, most grilled items, especially using this method, cook relatively quickly. Direct grilling creates a sear that caramelizes meats, providing texture and flavor. This is a major reason why everybody loves grilling so much—that beautiful char that is beyond golden brown but before burnt. When cooked perfectly, your meat, fish and vegetables will be roasted outside, moist and juicy inside.

To prepare for direct grilling with charcoal, spread an even layer of unlit charcoal (about one briquette or charcoal chunk deep) in the bottom of the grill. Then fill the chimney with charcoals and light it according to the instructions on page 14. When the coals in the chimney are hot, pour them over the unlit coals. In a gas grill, turn on the gas, then light the flame on both sides of the grill.

There are three areas of direct grilling. Each one is used for different processes. A low grill, in which you should be able to hold your hands about 5 inches/12.5cm over the fire for no more than 8 to 10 seconds, is good for recipes in which you want to give the inside time to cook but the fire is cool enough that the exterior doesn't burn. We see this in John and Andrea's Grilled Narragansett Pizza (page 87) and Delpha's Grilled Chicken Wings (page 95). We use a medium grill, which should be hot enough that you can only hold your hands over the fire for 5 to 8 seconds, for speed and flavor. With shrimp, for example, if the fire is too high, it will burn the outside before the inside is cooked. If it's too low, it will overcook the outside before the inside is cooked and you won't get caramelization. With thicker cuts—1 inch/2.5cm or more—such as lamb T-bones, a medium fire ensures the entire piece is cooked at the same time. A hot grill, where you can hold your hand over the fire for no more than 3 to 5 seconds, is where all the speed comes in. This is perfect for thinner items that cook relatively quickly, from burgers to steaks to fish fillets.

TWO-ZONE GRILLING

Two-zone grilling allows for a slow building of caramelization and an element of roasting. The food cooks with the heat from the coals as well as the ambient air and smoke generated when the cover is closed, without having the fire sear it directly. Most of the time, two-zone cooking is roasting, with the added benefit of radiant heat.

To prepare for two-zone grilling with a gas grill, turn on just one side of the grill. Depending on the recipe, you can watch the thermostat to achieve the desired temperature. Charcoal grilling presents a little more of a challenge because regulating the heat involves three things: the amount of lit coal, adding more coal and the amount of oxygen the fire gets. In most cases, you will be cooking in a covered grill, and most of the two-zone recipes in this book call for specific temperatures rather than low, medium or high fires.

To prepare the grill for two-zone cooking, pile charcoal against one side of the grill. Fill the chimney with charcoal, using newspaper to start the fire (see directions on the following page). Pour the lit charcoal over the unlit charcoal. One side of the grill will have an active fire going and the other side should have no charcoal at all. When the fire is hot (you should be able to hold your hands over it for 5 to 10 seconds), cover the grill. If the grill does not have a built-in temperature gauge, drop the probe of a remote thermometer through the top vent. For low heat, adjust the vents so they are three-quarters closed. For high heat, open the vents all the way. Follow cues in the recipe to determine when the grill is ready. Once the fire has reached the desired temperature, you have to monitor it pretty constantly—no stepping inside to watch the game—and be prepared with your ingredients and tools.

Although science is definitely involved, grilling is an art; it's a craft. Depending on the type of grill you have, you may have to remove the cover, carefully move the grate—sometimes with the food on it—and feed the fire by sprinkling coal and briquettes over the fire, being careful to use only a small amount so you don't kill the fire. Don't wait for the fire to die before doing this. Some grills have a hinged grate, which is perfect for this.

MAINTAINING GRILL TEMPERATURE

At Andy's restaurant in Boston, Tremont 647, the grill is the centerpiece, and if that fire ever goes out there will be a lot of unhappy customers. So cooks are continually feeding it all night. You won't be doing that for six hours, but maintaining the fire and regulating temperature are key. We are going to give you all the tips we can, but we can only get you so far. Only you can get to know your fire, and this takes lots of practice. The good news is that the practice is fun. And the results will be tasty at worst, spectacular at best.

OUR GO-TO COOKING METHODS

It is implicit in all of these methods that you start cooking with a clean grill.

HOW TO BUILD A LOW DIRECT FIRE

Spread an even layer of unlit charcoal in the bottom of the grill. Fill a chimney one-third full with charcoal. Stuff two sheets of newspaper in the bottom of the chimney and light it. When the coals are fully engaged—you should see flames peeking over the top—pour them over the unlit charcoal. When you can hold your hand over the fire for no more than 8 to 10 seconds, it is ready.

HOW TO BUILD A MEDIUM DIRECT FIRE

Spread an even layer of unlit charcoal in the bottom of the grill. Fill a chimney halfway with charcoal. Stuff two sheets of newspaper in the bottom of the chimney and light it. When the coals are fully engaged—you should see flames peeking over the top—pour them over the unlit charcoal. When you can hold your hand over the fire for no more than 5 to 8 seconds, it is ready.

HOW TO BUILD A HOT DIRECT FIRE

Spread an even layer of unlit charcoal in the bottom of the grill. Fill a chimney with charcoal. Stuff two sheets of newspaper in the bottom of the chimney and light it. When the coals are fully engaged—you should see flames peeking over the top—pour them over the unlit charcoal. When you can hold your hand over the fire for no more than 3 to 5 seconds, it is ready.

HOW TO BUILD A TWO-ZONE CHARCOAL FIRE

Prepare the grill for two-zone grilling. Pile the unlit charcoal on one side of the grill. Fill a chimney with charcoal. Stuff two sheets of newspaper in the bottom of the chimney and light it. When the coals are fully engaged—you should see flames peeking over the top—pour them over the unlit charcoal. Cover the grill. For a low fire, shut the vents 75 percent. When the temperature reaches 250°F to 300°F/121°C to 149°C, start cooking! For a hot fire, open the vents all the way. When the temperature reaches 350°F to 400°F/177°C to 204°C, you're ready to go.

Gas people, you have it easy. Light the gas and turn the knobs to adjust the temperature. You still have to control it, but the process is more similar to working with an indoor unit than with live fire. With charcoal you need to keep in mind that when the coals are at their apex, the fire is about to die. When professional chefs and seasoned grillers are cooking for long periods of time, this is when we load in more coal or wood, carefully removing the grate or sliding it to one side with heatproof gloves or pot holders, and evenly spreading charcoal across hot coals, being careful not to smother the fire. This will make the temperature drop, but it will come back full speed in no time.

The key is not to smother your fire. Instead, either pour the coals next to it or, using tongs or an offset metal spatula, pile the coals on one side and pour the coals next to the hot pile. This way as the fire dies the next pile will be raging. If you are using a low fire, it is best to sprinkle a little bit of charcoal over the hot coals, making sure not to smother the fire or increase the heat too much.

HOW TO BUILD A TWO-ZONE FIRE IN A GAS GRILL

Typically, burners in gas grills are arranged from front to back or side to side. The front-to-back arrangement is more common in grills with a rotisserie. Depending on the size of your surface, this may be more difficult for two-zone cooking. The more common setup is side-to-side burners, which is perfect for two-zone grilling.

To prepare your gas grill for two-zone grilling, turn on only one burner—if they are front to back, turn on the back one; if side to side, turn on whichever side is most comfortable for you. If you are lucky enough to have a three-burner grill, that is ideal for double-bank grilling, which we recommend for the Lemon and Fresh Herb Grill-Roasted Leg of Lamb, on page 158.

CHAPTER 1

SEAR IT:
HOT DIRECT GRILLING

Hot direct grilling is where it all began. This is how everybody learns to grill. It's the most frequently used technique outdoors as well as in professional kitchens. Hot direct grilling is all about the sear, caramelization and speed. When we sear the exterior of a beautiful piece of meat, for example, we are caramelizing its natural proteins and sugars. This is inherently what everybody loves in grilled food— that charred crunch we find in everything from pork belly to lamb T-bones to tuna steak when they are cooked over a hot fire.

TAMARI-GLAZED STEAK WITH SWEET-AND-SPICY RICE

SKIRT AND FLANK STEAKS ARE SOME OF OUR FAVORITES TO GRILL, BUT WHEN IT'S FANCY TIME WE GO FOR THE NEW YORK STRIP, A NICE 1-INCH/2.5CM-THICK CENTER CUT. YOU CAN'T GO WRONG WITH THIS. IT'S A LITTLE ON THE PRICEY SIDE, BUT IN OUR OPINION THE BEEF FLAVOR AND CHEW ARE SUPERIOR. LIKE SOY SAUCE, TAMARI IS MADE FROM FERMENTED SOYBEANS. BUT THIS JAPANESE CONDIMENT IS SLIGHTLY THICKER WITH A MORE COMPLEX, LESS SALTY FLAVOR. IT IS ALSO GLUTEN-FREE, WHICH IS AN ADVANTAGE FOR MANY PEOPLE.

THE KEY HERE IS TO BUILD AN EVEN, HIGH FIRE. IF IT'S TOO LOW, YOU WON'T GET THE CRUST THAT ROCKS PEOPLE'S WORLD. WITH THIS DISH YOU WANT A DEEP GOLDEN BROWN CRUST AND A PERFECT MEDIUM-RARE INSIDE. DON'T FORGET TO REST YOUR MEAT FOR 5 MINUTES AFTER COOKING IT. WE KNOW YOU'RE HUNGRY, BUT YOU'LL RUIN AN AWESOME STEAK BY CUTTING INTO IT TOO SOON BECAUSE ALL OF THE JUICES WILL RUN OUT.

WE FEEL IT'S REALLY IMPORTANT TO PULL OUR STEAKS OUT OF THE REFRIGERATOR 30 TO 40 MINUTES BEFORE STARTING TO COOK THEM. THIS WAY THEY TEMPER, MEANING THEY COME TO ROOM TEMPERATURE, AND COOK MORE EVENLY.

¼ cup/60ml tamari

¼ cup/60ml agave nectar or honey

2 tbsp/30ml rice wine vinegar

1 tbsp/12g sugar

½ tsp cayenne pepper

½ tsp ground white pepper

4 (12-oz/340g) center-cut New York strip steaks, about 1"/2.5cm thick

Kosher salt and freshly ground black pepper, to taste

Sticky Rice, for serving (recipe follows)

Sweet-and-Spicy Sauce, for serving (recipe follows)

Equipment: Wire rack set in a rimmed baking sheet, instant-read thermometer

Make the glaze: In a medium bowl, mix the tamari, agave, vinegar, sugar, cayenne and white pepper. Set aside.

Build a hot direct fire. Spread an even layer of unlit charcoal in the bottom of the grill. Fill a chimney with charcoal. Stuff two sheets of newspaper in the bottom of the chimney and light it. When the coals are fully engaged—you should see flames peeking over the top—pour them over the unlit charcoal. If using a gas grill, light the gas and adjust the temperature on both sides to high.

(continued)

When you can hold your hands over the fire for no more than 3 to 5 seconds, clean the grill grate. Season the steaks with salt and pepper and place on the grill. Cook for about 2½ minutes, then rotate 90 degrees and cook for about 2½ minutes more. At this point you should have a deep golden crust. Flip the steaks over and repeat. Using an instant-read thermometer, check the internal temperature. Steaks should be 125°F to 130°F/52°C to 54°C. Brush liberally with the glaze, flip over and caramelize for 20 seconds; repeat on the second side. Remove from the grill and place on a cooling rack set in a baking sheet for 5 minutes. If you have any glaze left, pour some over the steaks while they are resting, reserving some to drizzle just before serving.

Evenly distribute the rice among 4 to 6 plates, mounding the rice on each plate. Make a shallow well in each mound with the back of a spoon, and pour a liberal spoonful of the Sweet-and-Spicy Sauce into each, drizzling a little around the base. Slice the steak and arrange it in overlapping layers over the rice. Drizzle with any remaining glaze.

STICKY RICE

MAKES 6 CUPS/1200G RICE

3 cups/700g sushi rice
4½ cups/1070ml cold water

Rinse the sushi rice with cold water in a colander until the water is clear. Place in bowl and let sit for 15 minutes. Place the rice and the 4½ cups/1070ml water in a medium saucepan over medium-high heat and bring to a boil. Give it a quick stir, reduce the heat to low, cover and let simmer for 20 minutes, until soft.

Remove from the heat and let cool for 5 minutes before serving.

SWEET-AND-SPICY SAUCE

½ cup/100g sugar

¼ cup/60ml water

1 serrano or jalapeño pepper, stemmed
and minced, with seeds

1 small red onion, minced

¼ cup/60ml fresh lime juice

2 tbsp/30ml fish sauce

2 tbsp/10g cilantro leaves, chopped

In a small saucepan over high heat, bring the sugar, water and pepper to a boil, stirring frequently, until the sugar has dissolved. Remove from the heat, place in a small bowl and cool in the refrigerator. When thoroughly chilled, stir in the remaining ingredients. Set aside until rice is done.

NICK STELLINO'S GRILLED STEAK WITH COFFEE RUB

WE ARE PROUD TO CALL NICK STELLINO, CHEF, COOKBOOK AUTHOR AND HOST OF THE PBS SHOW *COOKING WITH NICK STELLINO*, OUR FRIEND. AND WE'RE THRILLED THAT HE LET US INCLUDE THIS EASY AND FABULOUS RECIPE.

DRY RUBS ARE ONE OF OUR FAVORITE WAYS TO ADD FLAVOR, AND THIS ONE IS SPECTACULAR BECAUSE IT ADDS TO THE FLAVOR OF AN ALREADY GREAT STEAK. YOU NEVER WANT TO APPLY A RUB MORE THAN 4 HOURS BEFORE YOU ARE READY TO COOK, BECAUSE THE SALT WILL START TO CURE THE MEAT. WHEN YOU ARE READY, WE SUGGEST LIGHTLY SPRINKLING THE RUB ON FIRST, THEN LIGHTLY PATTING IT. COME TO THINK OF IT, THE WORD *RUB* IS A BIT OF A MISNOMER BECAUSE WE ARE TRYING TO SEASON THE MEAT, NOT FORCE IT INTO THE CENTER.

---

1 tbsp/5g finely ground espresso coffee

1 tbsp/5g onion powder

1 tbsp/5g paprika

1 tsp salt

1 tsp pepper

1 tsp chili powder

1 tbsp/12g brown sugar

4 rib-eye steaks, approximately 12 oz/340g each

Make the coffee rub: In a small bowl, thoroughly combine everything but the steak.

If the steaks have been in the refrigerator, bring them to room temperature for 30 minutes to an hour. Pat them dry with paper towels, and coat them thoroughly on all sides with the rub. Refrigerate, covered, for at least 30 minutes and up to 4 hours.

Build a hot direct fire. Spread an even layer of unlit charcoal in the bottom of the grill. Fill a chimney with charcoal. Stuff two sheets of newspaper in the bottom of the chimney and light it. When the coals are fully engaged—you should see flames peeking over the top—pour them over the unlit charcoal. If using a gas grill, light the gas and adjust the temperature on both sides to high.

When you can hold your hands over the fire for no more than 3 to 5 seconds, clean the grill grate. Grill the steaks, covered, for about 4½ minutes. Flip the steaks and cook for another 4½ minutes, or until a thermometer registers 125°F/52°C for medium-rare. If you like your steaks more well done (but why would you?), cook for another minute or two. Transfer the steaks to a cutting board and let rest for 5 minutes before serving.

Nick Stellino
KING WITH FRIENDS

TWICE-COOKED NEW ENGLAND–STYLE STEAK TIP SKEWERS

FLAP MEAT, BY ANY OTHER NAME . . . HERE IN NEW ENGLAND, WE CALL 'EM STEAK TIPS (OR SIRLOIN TIPS), AND WE LOVE 'EM AS MUCH AS WE LOVE OUR RED SOX, PATRIOTS, BRUINS AND CELTICS. THIS DELICIOUS, INEXPENSIVE CUT IS PERFECT FOR SKEWERING AND GRILLING BECAUSE IT IS JUICY AND TENDER AND ABSORBS MARINADES BEAUTIFULLY.

WE'RE COMBINING A COUPLE OF METHODS HERE, GRILLING THE STEAK TIP SKEWERS AND VEGETABLES DIRECTLY OVER THE FIRE SEPARATELY, THEN FINISHING THE MEAT OFF THE SKEWERS—AGAIN OVER THE FIRE—IN A PAN WITH THE GRILLED VEGETABLES.

WE LIKE TO USE METAL SKEWERS FOR THIS RECIPE BECAUSE WE ARE DIRECT GRILLING. THEY WON'T BURN AND ARE REUSABLE.

---

3 lb/1360g sirloin tips, cut into approximately 2" to 3"/5cm to 7.6cm cubes

Kosher salt

2 cups/200g button mushrooms

1 sweet onion, cut into ½"/13mm-thick slices

Vegetable oil, for grilling

1 red bell pepper, halved, cored and seeded

½ cup/120ml Soy Sake Sauce (recipe follows)

8 cherry tomatoes, halved

Equipment: Eight 12"/30cm skewers, preferably metal; 12"/30cm cast-iron skillet, instant-read thermometer

Thread the sirloin tips onto skewers and season lightly with salt. Thread the whole button mushrooms onto skewers. Set aside.

Build a hot direct fire. Spread an even layer of unlit charcoal in the bottom of the grill. Fill a chimney with charcoal. Stuff two sheets of newspaper in the bottom of the chimney and light it. When the coals are fully engaged—you should see flames peeking over the top—pour them over the unlit charcoal. If using a gas grill, light the gas and adjust the temperature on both sides to high.

When you can hold your hands over the fire for no more than 3 to 5 seconds, clean the grill grate. Heat a large cast-iron pan over the fire for about 3 to 5 minutes. Wearing heatproof gloves, remove the pan from the fire and set aside on a heatproof surface.

Brush each side of the onion slices with oil and grill for 3 minutes per side. Cut each slice into quarters and transfer to the cast-iron pan.

Grill the pepper for 2 minutes per side, or until well charred. Cut each half into quarters and transfer to the cast-iron pan.

(continued)

Grill the steak skewers for 2 minutes per side or until a thermometer inserted into a piece registers 120ºF/49ºC. Remove the meat from the skewers and set on top of the grilled vegetables.

Grill the mushroom skewers for 2 minutes per side. Remove from the skewers and set on top of the meat. Drizzle the Soy Sake Sauce into the pan and add the cherry tomatoes. Toss to blend the ingredients. Place the cast-iron pan back on the grill for 3 to 4 minutes to warm. Serve immediately.

SOY SAKE SAUCE

MAKES 2 CUPS/475ML

½ cup/120ml soy sauce
½ cup/120ml sake
1 cup/240ml water
1 scallion, thinly sliced
2 tsp/3g red pepper flakes

In a small mixing bowl, combine all the ingredients and mix well. Cover and refrigerate for up to 1 week.

LAMB T-BONES AND MINT PISTOU

THE FRESH, BRIGHT FLAVORS OF THE PISTOU (A FRENCH VERSION OF ITALIAN PESTO, WITHOUT THE NUTS AND CHEESE) PAIRED WITH THE LAMB TAKE THIS DISH OVER THE TOP.

IT'S BEST TO BUY LAMB T-BONES THAT ARE AT LEAST 1 INCH/2.5CM THICK. LAMB HAS A TENDENCY TO FLARE UP DUE TO THE FAT ON THE OUTSIDE OF THE CHOP AS WELL AS THE MARINADE. KEEP AN EYE ON IT AND MOVE THE MEAT AROUND THE GRILL IF YOU SEE FLARE-UPS HAPPENING. A GOOD REST MAKES THE MEAT TENDER AND JUICY.

¼ cup/60ml olive oil

Juice and grated zest of 1 lemon

¼ cup/20g roughly chopped parsley leaves

2 cloves garlic, roughly chopped

1 sprig rosemary leaves, chopped

Kosher salt and freshly cracked black pepper, to taste

8 (1"/2.5cm thick) lamb T-bones, fat trimmed off side

Mint Pistou, for serving (recipe follows)

Equipment: Instant-read thermometer

Make the marinade: Place the olive oil, lemon juice and zest, parsley, garlic and rosemary in a food processor and purée until smooth. Stir in salt and pepper to taste. You want the marinade to be just a little too salty and peppery. Since you are not marinating the inside of the meat, the outside flavor has to be big and bold.

Rub the lamb all over with the marinade. Cover and refrigerate for 1 hour. Turn the lamb over and refrigerate for at least 1 and up to 8 hours more. This would be a good time to make the pistou.

Remove the meat from the refrigerator 30 minutes before you want to grill.

Build a hot direct fire. Spread an even layer of unlit charcoal in the bottom of the grill. Fill a chimney with charcoal. Stuff two sheets of newspaper in the bottom of the chimney and light it. When the coals are fully engaged—you should see flames peeking over the top—pour them over the unlit charcoal. If using a gas grill, light the gas and adjust the temperature on both sides to high.

(continued)

When you can hold your hands over the fire for no more than 3 to 5 seconds, clean the grill grate. Brush the marinade off the T-bones and place them in the center of the grill. Cook for 3 to 4 minutes, until the lamb is dark golden brown. Flip over and cook for another 3 to 4 minutes, until a thermometer inserted into the meat registers 130°F/54°C.

Let the lamb rest for 5 minutes on a wire rack. Transfer to a platter and drizzle the pistou over the meat, passing any that remains. We'd eat this all day with some grilled asparagus and polenta. Just sayin'.

MINT PISTOU

MAKES 1 CUP/240ML

1 cup/80g roughly chopped fresh mint leaves

½ cup/40g fresh parsley leaves

1 clove garlic

½ tsp red pepper flakes

½ cup/120ml olive oil

Kosher salt and freshly cracked black pepper, to taste

Place the mint, parsley, garlic and red pepper flakes in a food processor. Turn the motor on and add the oil in a slow, steady stream through the feed tube until you have a smooth, pourable paste. Transfer to a bowl and season with salt and pepper. Cover and refrigerate until ready to use.

GRILLED PORK BELLY GERMAN POTATO SALAD

THIS IS A PERFECT DISH TO MAKE A FEW DAYS AHEAD FOR A PICNIC OR PARTY; THOUGH IN OUR CASE, WE CAN NEVER WAIT. WE ALWAYS EAT IT RIGHT AWAY.

MOST TIMES WHEN GRILLING PORK BELLY WE USE THE SLOW METHOD. HERE WE COOK THE BELLY FAST AND FURIOUS. SINCE WE'RE GRILLING THIN STRIPS (YES, YOU CAN SUBSTITUTE BACON, IF YOU MUST), WE WANT TO HAVE A MEDIUM TO HIGH FIRE. THIS WILL CRISP UP THE MEAT AND ADD AN EXCELLENT CHARRED FLAVOR TO THE SALAD. AND YOU KNOW WE LOVE THAT CHARRED FLAVOR.

1½ lb/680g Yukon gold potatoes, washed, skin on, cut into ½"/13mm dice

2 tbsp/36g kosher salt

½ lb/230g pork belly, sliced into ¼"/6mm-thick strips

¼ cup/60ml aged sherry vinegar or cider vinegar

2 tbsp/30ml olive oil

1 tbsp/15g whole-grain mustard

2 tsp/6g rosemary leaves, minced

1 clove garlic, minced

2 scallions, cut into ¼"/6mm-thick rings

2 stalks celery, diced

¼ cup/20g parsley leaves, roughly chopped

Kosher salt and freshly ground pepper, to taste

Build a hot direct fire. Spread an even layer of unlit charcoal in the bottom of the grill. Fill a chimney with charcoal. Stuff two sheets of newspaper in the bottom of the chimney and light it. When the coals are fully engaged—you should see flames peeking over the top—pour them over the unlit charcoal. If using a gas grill, light gas and adjust the temperature on both sides to high.

Place the potatoes in a large saucepan, fill with just enough cold water to cover, add the kosher salt and place over high heat. When the water begins to boil, reduce the heat and simmer until the potatoes are fork-tender, about 8 to 10 minutes. When the potatoes are done, strain and run cold water over the potatoes until cool. Drain thoroughly and set aside.

When you can hold your hands over the fire for no more than 3 to 5 seconds, clean the grill grate. Carefully lay the pork belly strips perpendicular to the grate. Grill for about 30 seconds, then flip, using long tongs—there will be flare-ups. Repeat this process twice on each side. Remove the belly from the grill and transfer to a baking sheet to cool. We don't put it on paper towels to drain because we want those extra juices in our salad (mmmm, pork fat). Once the meat has cooled, cut the strips crosswise into ¼ inch/6mm pieces.

In a medium-size mixing bowl, whisk the vinegar, oil, mustard, rosemary and garlic until well blended. Add the cooked potatoes, pork belly, scallions, celery and parsley to the bowl, and very gently fold together. Season with salt and pepper and serve immediately, or refrigerate until needed, up to 3 days.

GRILLED SHRIMP, ROMAINE AND RADICCHIO SALAD

MAKES 4 TO 6 SERVINGS

GRILLING LETTUCE IS A FANTASTIC WAY TO ADD THOSE GREAT CHAR FLAVORS TO A SALAD. THE KEY IS TO SEAR THE LEAVES WITHOUT WILTING THEM TOO MUCH. LEAVE THIS FOR THE LAST MOMENT, AND THEY WILL STILL BE TENDER AND CRISP—AND CHARRED.

A PERFECTLY GRILLED SHRIMP SHOULD HAVE A SLIGHT SNAP TO IT AND BE SWEET AND JUICY. PAY ATTENTION TO THE SIDES OF THE SHRIMP TO SEE WHEN THEY CHANGE FROM TRANSLUCENT TO WHITE. THEY WILL CONTINUE TO COOK A BIT EVEN AFTER THEY'RE OFF THE GRILL, SO JUST BEFORE THEY ARE TOTALLY WHITE, PULL THEM OFF, LET STAND FOR A FEW SECONDS, THEN SERVE.

Juice of 2 lemons

⅓ cup/80ml olive oil

1 shallot, minced

¼ cup/20g chopped fresh parsley leaves

4 leaves fresh basil, roughly chopped

1 tsp red pepper flakes

Kosher salt and freshly ground black pepper, to taste

Olive oil, for grilling

8 to 12 shrimp (U-12), peeled and deveined

1 head romaine, outer leaves removed, quartered through the core (no need to cut off the end)

1 small head radicchio, loose leaves removed, quartered through the core (no need to cut off the end)

1 wedge (about 4 oz/113g) Parmesan or your favorite hard cheese, for garnish

Build a hot direct fire. Spread an even layer of unlit charcoal in the bottom of the grill. Fill a chimney with charcoal. Stuff two sheets of newspaper in the bottom of the chimney and light it. When the coals are fully engaged—you should see flames peeking over the top—pour them over the unlit charcoal. If using a gas grill, light the gas and adjust the temperature on both sides to high.

Make the vinaigrette: In a large bowl, whisk together the lemon juice, olive oil, shallot, parsley, basil and red pepper flakes. Season with salt and pepper. Set aside.

When you can hold your hands over the fire for no more than 3 to 5 seconds, clean the grill grate. Lightly oil the shrimp and season with salt and pepper. Grill for 1 minute, rotate 90 degrees and then flip. Continue to cook for 1 to 2 minutes more until the outer skin is pinkish red with a slight char on it and the split side has just turned from translucent to white. Remove the shrimp from the grill, place in the vinaigrette bowl and toss.

Make the salad: Lightly oil the romaine and radicchio and season with salt and pepper. Place the romaine quarters on the grill and cook for 1 minute per side (there are 3 sides), until it is slightly charred and lightly warmed. Transfer to a cutting board and roughly chop the leaves; discard the cores. Scatter the leaves over the serving plate. Repeat with the radicchio, and scatter the leaves over the romaine.

Spoon the shrimp in the vinaigrette evenly over the lettuces. Using a vegetable peeler, shave some Parmesan over the salad. Serve immediately.

CURRIED CHICKEN TENDERLOINS WITH COCONUT AND PAPAYA SALAD

THE COMBINATION OF SWEET AND SPICY CHICKEN, CRUNCHY COCONUT AND A CARIBBEAN-INFLECTED SALAD MAKES THIS DISH ABSOLUTELY ADDICTIVE. CHICKEN TENDERLOINS ARE THE PERFECT TWO- OR THREE-BITE MEAT, REALLY COST-EFFECTIVE AND—WHEN DONE RIGHT—JUICY AND TENDER. THE PROBLEM IS THE TENDON THAT YOU HAVE TO REMOVE. THIS IS TRICKY AND TAKES SOME PRACTICE. WE CAN HELP.

TO REMOVE THE TENDON, FIRST FIND ITS WHITE TIP, STICKING OUT OF THE FAT END OF THE TENDER. PINCH IT BETWEEN YOUR THUMB AND FOREFINGER AND HOLD IT FIRMLY AGAINST THE CUTTING BOARD (YOU MAY WANT TO USE A PAPER TOWEL; IT GETS SLIPPERY). PLACE THE TIP OF A PARING KNIFE JUST BEYOND YOUR FINGER, BETWEEN THE TENDON AND THE MEAT, AND USE A LIGHT SAWING MOTION TO PUSH THE MEAT AWAY FROM YOU, SLIDING IT OFF THE TENDON. IT'S NOT AS TOUGH AS IT SOUNDS, WE PROMISE.

---

1 cup/240g Greek-style yogurt

Juice and zest of 1 lime

2 tbsp/30ml red wine vinegar

1 tbsp/5g minced fresh ginger

2 cloves garlic, minced

2 tsp/4g garam masala

2 tsp/4g kosher salt

2 tsp/4g ground black pepper

1 tsp curry powder

2 lb/900g chicken tenderloins, tendons removed

Coconut and Papaya Salad (recipe follows)

Make the marinade: In a large bowl, thoroughly mix all the ingredients except the chicken and salad.

Toss the chicken in the marinade to coat thoroughly. Cover and refrigerate for 2 to 4 hours.

Build a hot direct fire. Spread an even layer of unlit charcoal in the bottom of the grill. Fill a chimney with charcoal. Stuff two sheets of newspaper in the bottom of the chimney and light it. When the coals are fully engaged—you should see flames peeking over the top—pour them over the unlit charcoal. If using a gas grill, light the gas and adjust the temperature on both sides to high.

(continued)

When you can hold your hands over the fire for no more than 3 to 5 seconds, clean the grill grate. Place the tenderloins perpendicular to the bars and cook for 1 to 2 minutes. The goal is to get a good sear without burning the meat. Once the marinade and chicken start to caramelize, flip the chicken and continue to cook. Repeat this process so the chicken cooks twice on both sides, for a total of 4 to 8 minutes (depending on the thickness of the tenderloins). Tenderloins are done when they are deep golden brown to lightly charred and have an internal temperature of 165°F/74°C. Serve immediately over the salad, or cool and serve cold with the salad.

COCONUT AND PAPAYA SALAD

MAKES 2 ENTRÉE OR 4 APPETIZER SERVINGS

2 ripe papayas, peeled, seeded and diced

1 medium red onion, julienned

1 red bell pepper, cored, seeded and diced

½ cup/120ml coconut cream or unsweetened coconut milk

Juice and minced zest of 2 limes

¼ cup/20g cilantro leaves, roughly chopped

1 jalapeño pepper, stemmed, seeded and minced

1 tbsp/12g sugar

1 tbsp/5g peeled and minced fresh ginger

1 tsp coriander seed, toasted and ground

1 tbsp/15ml olive oil

Kosher salt and freshly cracked black pepper, to taste

¼ cup/25g unsweetened coconut flakes, toasted to golden brown

In a bowl, combine the papaya, onion, bell pepper, coconut cream, lime juice and zest, cilantro, jalapeño, sugar, ginger, coriander and oil. Season with salt and pepper and set aside. (Cover and refrigerate if you are using it the next day.) Just before serving, sprinkle the toasted coconut on top.

GRILLED SPAM LOCO MOCO WITH CURRIED SLAW

MAKES 4 SERVINGS

YES, SPAM! IT GETS A BAD RAP, BUT WE REALLY DO LOVE IT. WHEN COOKED RIGHT, IT GETS A WONDERFUL, CRUNCHY EXTERIOR AND A CREAMY CENTER. THINK OF IT AS OLD-SCHOOL CHARCUTERIE. TELL YOUR FRIENDS YOU GOT IT AT THE NEW BUTCHER EVERYONE'S TALKING ABOUT AND YOU'LL GET RAVES. THEN PULL OUT THE CAN AT THE END AND YELL, "SPAM!" IF ANYBODY IS CURIOUS, LOCO MOCO IS A POPULAR HAWAIIAN MEAL THAT TYPICALLY INCLUDES WHITE RICE TOPPED WITH A HAMBURGER, A FRIED EGG AND GRAVY. VARIATIONS CAN FEATURE A HOST OF MEATS, INCLUDING OUR FAVORITE, SPAM.

AS WITH ALL DIRECT-FIRE COOKING, YOU HAVE TO WATCH OUT FOR BURNING. SPAM, LIKE ANY SAUSAGE, HAS A HIGH FAT-TO-MEAT RATIO, WHICH MAKES IT PARTICULARLY SUSCEPTIBLE TO FLARE-UPS. MAKE SURE YOUR GRILL IS VERY CLEAN AND FLIP THE MEAT AS SOON AS YOU SEE A NICE CHAR.

---

2 cups/475ml Curried Slaw (recipe follows)

1 cup/240ml Island Barbecue Sauce, warm (recipe follows)

2 cups/475ml Grilled Onion Gravy, hot (recipe follows)

1 can (12 oz/340g) Spam

Vegetable oil for grilling

4 eggs

4 cups/950g steamed white rice

1 tomato, chopped

¼ cup/20g minced parsley

You can make the Curried Slaw, Island Barbecue Sauce and Grilled Onion Gravy up to 3 days before serving.

Build a hot direct fire. Spread an even layer of unlit charcoal in the bottom of the grill. Fill a chimney with charcoal. Stuff two sheets of newspaper in the bottom of the chimney and light it. When the coals are fully engaged—you should see flames peeking over the top—pour them over the unlit charcoal. If using a gas grill, light the gas and adjust the temperature on both sides to high.

While the fire is heating, slice the Spam into eight ½ inch/13mm slices and brush them with oil. When you can hold your hands over the fire for no more than 3 to 5 seconds, clean the grill grate. Grill the Spam for 3 minutes, turn it over and grill 3 minutes more. Brush with barbecue sauce, turn over and grill 1 minute. Brush the second side with sauce, turn and grill 1 minute more, until the Spam is sticky and slightly charred around the edges.

Fry the eggs, and while they are cooking, mound 1 cup/240g cooked rice in each of 4 bowls. Ladle the hot Grilled Onion Gravy over the rice in each bowl. Place 2 slices of Spam and a fried egg on top of the rice, and sprinkle the dish with the tomato and minced parsley. Add a scoop of Curried Slaw on the side.

CURRIED SLAW

4 cups/280g shredded cabbage

1 large carrot, peeled and shredded

2 scallions, sliced

½ cup/75g golden raisins

¼ cup/60ml olive oil

2 tbsp/30ml rice wine vinegar

1 tbsp/15ml fresh lime juice (from about ½ lime)

1 tbsp/15ml agave nectar or honey

6 mint leaves, cut into chiffonade

1 tsp curry powder

1 tsp black poppy seeds

1 tsp kosher salt

½ tsp ground white pepper

In a large bowl, mix the cabbage, carrot, scallions and raisins. In a small bowl, whisk together the remaining ingredients. Pour the dressing over the cabbage mixture. Mix well, cover and refrigerate overnight or up to 3 days.

ISLAND BARBECUE SAUCE

½ cup/120g brown sugar

½ cup/120ml apple cider vinegar

2 tbsp/10g minced fresh ginger

1 tbsp/5g garlic powder

1 tsp curry powder

½ tsp Chinese five-spice powder

1 cup/240ml pineapple juice

1 cup/240ml ketchup

In a large saucepan over medium heat, bring the brown sugar and vinegar to a simmer. Add the ginger, garlic powder, curry powder and Chinese five-spice powder, and simmer for 10 minutes, whisking often. Add the pineapple juice and ketchup. Simmer for 30 minutes more, whisking occasionally. Keeps for up to 1 month in the refrigerator.

GRILLED ONION GRAVY

MAKES 1½ CUPS/350ML

1 large sweet onion, cut into ½"/
13mm-thick slices

1 large portobello mushroom cap

Kosher salt and freshly ground black
pepper, to taste

1 tbsp/15g butter

½ tbsp/7.5g flour

2 cups/475ml beef stock or beef broth,
at room temperature

2 tbsp/30ml Worcestershire sauce

1 tsp onion powder

1 tsp garlic powder

Build a hot direct fire (following directions above). When you can hold your hands over the fire for no more than 3 to 5 seconds, season the onion and mushroom with salt and pepper and grill for 3 to 4 minutes per side. Remove from the grill and coarsely chop. Place the butter and flour in a medium saucepan and set on the grill. When the butter melts, stir constantly to blend, about 1 minute. Add the broth, Worcestershire sauce, onions and mushroom to the gravy and bring to a simmer. Cook, stirring occasionally, until thickened, about 15 minutes. Stir in onion and garlic powders and season with salt and pepper. Refrigerate for up to 3 days.

SEARED GREENS WITH GRILLED CHICKEN LIVERS AND BLUE CHEESE

MAKES 4 TO 6 SERVINGS

TANGY BLUE CHEESE IS A PERFECT FOIL FOR EARTHY SEARED GREENS. WHEN GRILLING LIVERS, WE FIND IT IS BEST TO SKEWER THEM. THEY ARE VERY SLIPPERY WHEN RAW AND CAN SLIP THROUGH THE GRILL GRATES EASILY. IF USING WOOD SKEWERS, BE SURE TO SOAK THEM IN WATER FIRST, SO THEY DON'T CATCH FIRE.

1 lb/450g chicken livers, trimmed and cut into chunks if large

Vegetable oil

2 tbsp/10g coarsely ground black pepper

1½ tsp/9g kosher salt

1 red onion, cut into ½"/13mm-thick slices

1 lemon, cut in half

1 tbsp/15ml olive oil

2 lb/900g beet greens or Swiss chard, washed well, stems trimmed, coarsely chopped

1 tsp red pepper flakes

⅓ cup/80ml red wine vinegar

4 oz/113g blue cheese (splurge on the good stuff; don't buy pre-crumbled)

Equipment: Twelve 8"/20cm skewers, 12"/30cm cast-iron pan

Thread the livers onto the skewers, brush with vegetable oil, rub with the black pepper and sprinkle with the salt. Set aside.

Build a hot direct fire. Spread an even layer of unlit charcoal in the bottom of the grill. Fill a chimney with charcoal. Stuff two sheets of newspaper in the bottom of the chimney and light it. When the coals are fully engaged—you should see flames peeking over the top—pour them over the unlit charcoal. If using a gas grill, light the gas and adjust the temperature on both sides to high.

When you can hold your hands over the fire for no more than 3 to 5 seconds, clean the grill grate. Grill the onion for 2 to 3 minutes per side, until slightly charred. Set aside.

Grill the livers for 3 minutes per side until well charred on the exterior and still medium-rare (pink) inside, about 140ºF/60ºC. Do not overcook them. Remove the livers and set aside with the onion. Squeeze lemon over the livers.

Heat a 12 inch/30cm cast-iron pan over the fire. When it's hot (a drop of water should sizzle and evaporate almost immediately), add the olive oil, then the greens, and sear, stirring occasionally, for 1 to 2 minutes, until they begin to wilt. Add the red pepper flakes and vinegar and cook, stirring, for 1 minute.

Divide the greens among 4 or 6 serving plates. Top with the livers and some of the grilled onion rings. Place the sliced or coarsely crumbled blue cheese on top. Drizzle each dish with some of the vinegar remaining in the pan.

ERIC'S MOLASSES-CHIPOTLE GLAZED SWEET POTATOES

MAKES 4 TO 8 SIDE-DISH SERVINGS

THIS IS A GO-TO DISH AT ANDREA'S HOUSE WHENEVER HER HUSBAND, ERIC, TAKES OVER GRILLING DUTIES. MOLASSES IS A BEAUTIFUL BASE FOR GLAZE TO BRUSH ON MANY GRILLED ITEMS. IT ADDS A SWEET, STICKY COATING THAT PROVIDES AN IDEAL CONTRAST TO THE SMOKE. ONE OF OUR FAVORITE TRICKS IS TO COAT A MEASURING CUP WITH VEGETABLE OIL BEFORE ADDING THE MOLASSES, TO MAKE IT POUR OUT EASILY.

4 medium-size sweet potatoes or yams, about 10 oz/284g each

1½ tbsp/22g butter

¼ cup/60ml molasses

¼ cup/60ml orange juice

1 tbsp/15ml light agave nectar or honey

1 tsp chipotle powder

¼ tsp cinnamon

Olive oil, for brushing

Kosher salt and freshly ground black pepper, to taste

Build a hot direct fire. Spread an even layer of unlit charcoal in the bottom of the grill. Fill a chimney with charcoal. Stuff two sheets of newspaper in the bottom of the chimney and light it. When the coals are fully engaged—you should see flames peeking over the top—pour them over the unlit charcoal. If using a gas grill, light the gas and adjust the setting on both sides to high.

Microwave the sweet potatoes until a fork can penetrate with slight resistance, approximately 6 minutes on high power, turning over once. Let cool.

In a small saucepan over medium heat, melt the butter. Add the molasses, orange juice and agave nectar, stirring gently until blended. Add the chipotle powder and cinnamon and stir until combined. Turn the heat down and simmer over medium-low for at least 15 minutes, or until ready to use.

Slice the sweet potatoes in half and brush lightly all over with the olive oil. Season with salt and pepper.

When you can hold your hands over the fire for no more than 3 to 5 seconds, clean the grill grate. Place the sweet potatoes flesh-side down on the grate and grill for approximately 3 minutes. (There should be grill marks on the flesh side.) Flip the potatoes and grill for another 3 minutes. Brush the glaze on the flesh sides and flip again, grilling flesh-side down for 1 minute. Lightly brush the skin side with the glaze and turn the potatoes over. Grill for 1 minute more, while brushing additional glaze on the flesh side. Flip again and grill for 30 seconds, then remove from the grill.

Serve immediately or cover loosely with aluminum foil to serve warm or at room temperature, passing any remaining glaze as a sauce.

Onions grill directly over fire

CHARRED SPRING VEGETABLES

WHEN WE GRILL VEGETABLES—WHICH IS AS OFTEN AS POSSIBLE—WE USUALLY DO IT ONE AT A TIME, BECAUSE THEY DO NOT ALL COOK AT THE SAME SPEED. WE DON'T WANT TO NAME NAMES, BUT TOO OFTEN WE SEE PEOPLE CROWD THEIR GRILLS. THIS CAN KEEP OXYGEN FROM GETTING TO THE FIRE, ULTIMATELY LEADING IT TO DIE DOWN IF YOU'RE NOT PAYING VERY CLOSE ATTENTION.

WE LIKE TO KEEP THE PREPARATION AS SIMPLE AS POSSIBLE, TO LET THE VEGETABLES' NATURAL FLAVORS SHINE THROUGH, BUT LEMON ZEST AND SMOKED PAPRIKA ADD A NICE KICK. THIS DISH IS MEANT TO BE SERVED AT ROOM TEMPERATURE BUT IS FANTASTIC CHILLED AS WELL. FEEL FREE TO MAKE IT THE DAY BEFORE YOU PLAN TO SERVE IT.

3 or 4 radishes, thinly sliced

6 tbsp/90ml olive oil, divided

3 young spring onions or 3 small yellow onions, peeled

8 carrots, preferably heirloom variety, peeled and cut about 4"/10cm long and 1"/2.5cm thick

1 bunch asparagus, thick ends removed

1 tsp kosher salt

1 tsp ground black pepper

½ tsp red pepper flakes

1 tsp smoked paprika (optional)

2 tsp/3g lemon zest

Build a hot direct fire. Spread an even layer of unlit charcoal in the bottom of the grill. Fill a chimney with charcoal. Stuff two sheets of newspaper in the bottom of the chimney and light it. When the coals are fully engaged—you should see flames peeking over the top—pour them over the unlit charcoal. If using a gas grill, light the gas and adjust the temperature on both sides to high.

In a large stainless steel bowl, toss the radishes with 1 tablespoon/15ml of the olive oil.

When you can hold your hands over the fire for no more than 3 to 5 seconds, clean the grill grate. Set a large cast-iron pan directly over the fire to heat for 3 to 5 minutes. When a droplet of water sizzles, the pan is ready. Cook the radishes for 2 minutes, stirring occasionally. Remove the pan from the grill and set aside.

Toss the onions in the bowl with another 1 tablespoon/15ml olive oil. Grill the onions directly over the fire until charred on all sides, about 5 minutes. Slice lengthwise into quarters and transfer to the pan with the radishes. Toss the carrots in the bowl with 1 tablespoon/15ml of the olive oil. Set crosswise on the grill grates and grill for about 3 to 5 minutes, until charred on all sides but still a bit raw. Place the carrots in the cast-iron pan. Repeat with the asparagus and 1 tablespoon/15ml oil, grilling for 3 to 4 minutes. Season the charred vegetables with salt, black pepper, red pepper flakes, paprika and the remaining 2 tablespoons/30ml olive oil. Stir gently, and return the pan to the grill for a few minutes until the vegetables are warm. Transfer all the vegetables to a clean bowl and sprinkle with the lemon zest. Toss and serve.

SEAR IT
APPETIZERS

BRENDAN'S CHAMPIONSHIP TUNA

MAKES 6 APPETIZER SERVINGS

WHEN WE COMPETE ON THE BARBECUE CIRCUIT, WE SOMETIMES GET BEATEN BY SOME REALLY GREAT COOKS. BRENDAN BUREK IS ONE OF THEM. WE HAVE SEEN HIM WIN WITH THIS DISH A FEW TIMES. THIS TRIPTYCH OF KILLER RECIPES—WASABI-COATED TUNA, SWEET ONION CORN CAKES AND AVOCADO SALAD—WILL TOTALLY WOW YOUR FRIENDS AND NEIGHBORS. EACH ELEMENT IS AWESOME ON ITS OWN, BUT TOGETHER THEY FORM A PERFECT UNION.

WE TRY TO GET A PERFECT SEAR ON THE OUTSIDE OF THE TUNA WHILE KEEPING THE INSIDE RARE. IT'S BEST TO HAVE THE STEAK CUT INTO CUBES WHENEVER POSSIBLE. IF YOUR PIECE IS NOT VERY THICK, WATCH CAREFULLY AND REDUCE YOUR COOKING TIME.

1 cup/240ml olive oil

½ cup/120ml soy sauce

1 tbsp/5g ground ginger

1 tsp onion powder

1 tsp garlic powder

½ tsp sesame oil

1½ tsp/7.5g ground black pepper, divided

1 lb/450g tuna steak, cut into six 2"/ 5cm cubes

1 cup/150g wasabi peas

1 tsp kosher salt

Sweet Onion Corn Cakes (recipe follows)

Wasabi Avocado Salad (recipe follows)

In a 1-gallon/3.8L plastic zipper bag, combine the olive oil, soy sauce, ginger, onion and garlic powders, sesame oil and ½ tsp of the black pepper. Shake to incorporate the ingredients. Place the tuna pieces in the bag and refrigerate for 1 to 2 hours.

In a spice grinder, combine the wasabi peas, salt and remaining 1 tsp pepper. Pulse until the peas are reduced to a fine powder. Transfer to a shallow bowl.

Build a hot direct fire. Spread an even layer of unlit charcoal in the bottom of the grill. Fill a chimney with charcoal. Stuff two sheets of newspaper in the bottom of the chimney and light it. When the coals are fully engaged—you should see flames peeking over the top—pour them over the unlit charcoal. If using a gas grill, light the gas and adjust the temperature on both sides to high.

While the fire is coming to temperature, remove the tuna from the marinade, shaking off any excess. Pat dry with paper towels. One at a time, coat the pieces with the wasabi pea rub and transfer to a clean plate.

When you can hold your hands over the fire for no more than 3 to 5 seconds, clean the grill grate. Lay the tuna pieces across the grate and grill for about 1 minute, then flip the pieces. Grill for 1 minute more. Transfer to a platter, and allow to rest for 5 minutes. The interior should be very rare with the center approaching raw. Slice the tuna ¼ inch/6mm thick and arrange on top of the corn cakes and salad.

SWEET ONION CORN CAKES

MAKES 1 CUP/240ML

2 or 3 ears corn

½ cup/100g chopped Vidalia onion

½ cup/60g flour

3 tbsp/15g chopped flat-leaf parsley

1 tbsp/5g chopped chives

¾ tsp kosher salt

½ tsp ground pepper

1 egg

⅓ cup/80ml milk

Oil for frying

Build a hot direct fire (see directions on page 49). Grill the corn directly over the fire, turning occasionally, until about one-quarter of the kernels are charred, 3 to 5 minutes. Cool slightly, then scrape the kernels from cobs.

In a large bowl, stir together the corn, onion, flour, parsley, chives, salt and pepper. Beat the egg and milk together, and add to the bowl. Stir until evenly mixed to form a loose, chunky batter.

Set a cast-iron pan on the grill and fill it about ½ inch/13mm deep with oil. When the oil is hot (a teaspoon of batter will crackle when added), drop large spoonfuls of batter into the oil, working in batches to avoid crowding the pan. You should use about ¼ cup/60ml for each cake.

Flip the cakes when golden brown, after about 3 minutes. Cook another 3 minutes. Be careful not to let them get too dark, or they will become chewy and tough.

Remove the cakes from the oil and drain on paper towels. Serve immediately.

WASABI AVOCADO SALAD

¼ cup/60ml fresh lime juice

2 scallions, chopped

3 tbsp/45ml soy sauce

2 tbsp/30ml canola oil

2 tsp/8g sugar

2 tsp/6g wasabi powder mixed with 2 tsp/10ml water

2 tsp/6g freshly grated ginger

½ avocado, pitted and thinly sliced

½ small red onion, peeled and thinly sliced

In a small jar, combine the lime juice, scallions, soy sauce, oil, sugar, wasabi paste and ginger. Shake to mix.

In a large bowl, toss the avocado and onion with the dressing. Top each corn cake with some salad, then place the sliced tuna on top.

SWEET, SPICY, SMOKY GRILLED SHRIMP COCKTAIL WITH CHIPOTLE SAUCE

PROFESSIONAL CHEFS KNOW THE FIRM FEELING OF A COOKED SHRIMP, WHICH IS SOMETHING THAT'S VALUABLE AND RELATIVELY EASY TO LEARN. GET TO KNOW THE FEEL OF RAW SHRIMP FIRST BY PUSHING DOWN ON THE THICKEST PART. THEN GRILL IT FOR A FEW MINUTES AND AFTER YOU HAVE FLIPPED IT, FEEL IT IN THE SAME PLACE. LET IT COOK FOR 2 TO 3 MINUTES MORE, THEN FEEL IT AGAIN. WHEN IT'S DONE IT SHOULD HAVE A SLIGHT SPRING TO IT BUT NOT BE SUPER FIRM. TO DOUBLE-CHECK YOUR WORK, CUT OFF A SMALL PIECE AT THE END AND LOOK AT THE INSIDE. IT SHOULD BE WHITE ALL THE WAY THROUGH AND STILL MOIST. YOU CAN ALSO CHECK THE TEMPERATURE. THE SHRIMP SHOULD BE ABOUT 140ºF/60ºC.

THE BRINE HERE IS PERFECT FOR SHRIMP—AND MOST SEAFOOD, FOR THAT MATTER. WE USE IT TO HELP CREATE FLAVOR AND KEEP THE SEAFOOD FROM DRYING OUT ON THE GRILL.

---

2 cups/475ml water

¼ cup/60g kosher salt

2 tbsp/25g sugar

12 U-8 (under 8 per lb) raw shrimp, peeled and deveined

½ cup/120ml ketchup

1 tbsp/15ml prepared horseradish

1 tbsp/15ml fresh lemon juice

1 tbsp/15ml minced chipotles in adobo sauce

2 tsp/10ml Memphis-Style Dry Rub (page 146) or your favorite dry rub

Make the brine: In a small saucepan, bring the water, salt and sugar to a simmer, stirring to dissolve. Pour the brine into a large bowl and cool to room temperature. Refrigerate, covered, for at least 2 hours.

Add the shrimp to the brine and refrigerate for 30 minutes.

While the shrimp are brining, make the cocktail sauce. In a small bowl, mix the ketchup, horseradish, lemon juice and chipotles in adobo sauce. Cover and set aside. If you won't be using the sauce right away, refrigerate until ready to use.

Build a hot direct fire. Spread an even layer of unlit charcoal in the bottom of the grill. Fill a chimney with charcoal. Stuff two sheets of newspaper in the bottom of the chimney and light it. When the coals are fully engaged—you should see flames peeking over the top—pour them over the unlit charcoal. If using a gas grill, light the gas and adjust the temperature on both sides to high.

(continued)

Rinse the shrimp under cold water and dry very well with paper towels. Lightly sprinkle with the dry rub.

When you can hold your hands over the fire for no more than 3 to 5 seconds, clean the grill grate. Grill the shrimp for 3 minutes. Flip and grill for an additional 2 minutes. Transfer the shrimp to a sheet pan and place in the freezer for 10 minutes, or until cool. Cover and refrigerate until ready to serve.

Serve the shrimp on a bed of crushed ice with the cocktail sauce on the side.

GRILL-ROASTED GINGER CLAMS WITH SAKE AND SCALLIONS

MAKES 4 APPETIZER OR 2 ENTRÉE SERVINGS

WE SHOT A LOT OF THE PHOTOS FOR OUR BURGER BOOK ON CAPE COD IN THE SUMMER, AND CHRIS BROUGHT HIS FAMILY ALONG FOR THE FUN. AS A REWARD FOR A HARD DAY OF EATING BURGERS, HE TOOK HIS KIDS CLAMMING IN WELLFLEET WITH THE WONDERFUL WOODBURY FAMILY, KNOWN FOR "PAT'S CLAMS" (YES, YOU CAN ORDER THEM ONLINE). THEIR HAUL INSPIRED THIS DISH.

HERE WE USE THE GRILL AS A STOVE. WHEN THE WEATHER IS NICE, WE LIKE TO BE OUTSIDE AS MUCH AS POSSIBLE, AND THIS IS A GREAT APPETIZER TO MAKE QUICKLY ON THE GRILL WHILE YOU ARE PREPARING FOR THE MAIN FEAST. YOU CAN MAKE THIS ON AN INDOOR STOVE, TOO, IF YOU MUST.

---

1 cup/240ml sake (dry white wine will work in a pinch)

1 tbsp/15ml chili garlic paste, sambal, or Sriracha

1 tbsp/15ml soy sauce

1 tbsp/15ml olive oil

1 tbsp/15ml sesame oil

16 littleneck clams, washed well to remove all sand

2 tbsp/10g minced fresh ginger

1 tbsp/5g minced garlic

Freshly ground black pepper, to taste

¼ cup/20g cilantro leaves

2 scallions, cut into ¼"/6mm-thick rings

1 lime, quartered

Equipment: 12"/30cm cast-iron pan

Build a hot direct fire. Spread an even layer of unlit charcoal in the bottom of the grill. Fill a chimney with charcoal. Stuff two sheets of newspaper in the bottom of the chimney and light it. When the coals are fully engaged—you should see flames peeking over the top—pour them over the unlit charcoal. If you are using a gas grill, light the gas and adjust the temperature on both sides to high.

In a small bowl, combine the sake, chili paste and soy sauce, and set aside.

When you can hold your hands over the fire for no more than 3 to 5 seconds, clean the grill grate. In a cast-iron pan, heat the oils on the grill. When the oil is hot (it will ripple and move quickly around the pan when tilted), add the clams and cook, stirring occasionally, for 2 minutes. Add the ginger and garlic and continue to cook, stirring, for 1 minute or until the ginger and garlic start to brown.

Add the sake mixture and cover the pan with a lid or baking sheet. Allow the clams to steam for 6 to 8 minutes, giving the pan a shake every minute or so, keeping the lid on. After 6 minutes, take a peek. If the clams are not open, continue cooking.

Once the clams are all open (there may be a few that never do; discard those), season with the pepper and sprinkle with the cilantro and scallions. Squeeze the lime wedges over the pan and bring it to your friends away from the grill so you can focus on the next course.

CHAPTER 2

ROASTING FOR FLAVOR: MEDIUM DIRECT GRILLING

Medium direct grilling is similar to roasting, but without the encapsulated heat. The fire is slightly higher than with low direct grilling—you should be able to hold your hand over it for 5 to 8 seconds—but not charring hot. Medium heat will still caramelize the meat or fish but won't overcook it before the interior is done. This is a perfect technique for items like Grilled King Salmon (page 61), Wood-Roasted Pork Tenderloin (page 77) and Beef and Asparagus Roulade (page 80), which have a tendency to dry out if cooked over heat that is too high or cooked too long over low heat.

GRILLED KING SALMON WITH ENGLISH PEAS AND MINT

MAKES 4 SERVINGS

ANDY GREW UP IN SEATTLE, AND AS FAR AS HE'S CONCERNED THERE IS NOTHING BETTER THAN KING SALMON (ALSO KNOWN AS CHINOOK SALMON) FROM PUGET SOUND. IT IS THE BIGGEST, AND SOME SAY THE BEST-TASTING, SALMON IN THE WORLD. ON THE GRILL, WITH A SIMPLE GARLIC BUTTER AND LEMON, IT CAN ROCK YOUR WORLD. IN THE SPRING, WHEN WE CAN GET FRESH PEAS, WE LOVE THIS PREPARATION.

TWO OF THE MOST COMMON ISSUES THAT COME UP WHEN GRILLING FISH ARE ITS PROCLIVITY TO STICK TO THE GRATES AND TO DRY OUT. THESE ARE EASILY ADDRESSED WITH PATIENCE AND KNOWING WHEN IT IS DONE. FOR SALMON, WE WANT AN INTERNAL TEMPERATURE OF 140ºF/60ºC—A NICE SOFT PINK ON THE INSIDE. PROFESSIONAL COOKS CAN TELL BY TOUCH, FEELING THE SPRING, OR GIVE, TO KNOW WHETHER FISH IS DONE. THIS TAKES PRACTICE, AND YOUR REWARD IS A GREAT SENSE OF ACCOMPLISHMENT WHEN YOU MASTER IT.

---

2 tbsp/30ml olive oil, plus more for fish

2 cloves garlic, minced

2 cups/300g blanched English peas or frozen peas, thawed

2 cups/475ml whole milk

30 leaves fresh mint

1 tbsp/15ml whole-grain mustard

Tabasco sauce, to taste

Kosher salt and freshly ground black pepper

4 (6-oz/170g) salmon fillets, skinned and deboned

Build a medium direct fire. Spread an even layer of unlit charcoal in the bottom of the grill. Fill a chimney halfway with charcoal. Stuff two sheets of newspaper in the bottom of the chimney and light it. When the coals are fully engaged—you should see flames peeking over the top—pour them over the unlit charcoal. If using a gas grill, light the gas and adjust the temperature on both sides to medium.

Make the sauce: In a small saucepan, combine the olive oil and garlic over medium-low heat, stirring, for 2 to 4 minutes, until the garlic is dark brown. Remove the pan from the heat and cool to room temperature. Transfer the garlic and oil to a blender. Add the peas, milk and mint, and purée on high until smooth. Transfer the purée to a small bowl and stir in the mustard. Season with Tabasco, salt and pepper. Refrigerate until needed, up to 1 day in advance.

(continued)

When you can hold your hands over the fire for no more than 5 to 8 seconds, clean the grill grate. Lightly brush the salmon fillets with olive oil, and season with salt and pepper. Grill for 2 minutes. *It is very important not to move the fish. If you move it too soon, or if the grill grates were not hot enough, the flesh will tear when you move it.* Once a sear has developed, rotate the fillets 90 degrees and grill for 1 minute more. Flip the fillets and repeat the process, until a thermometer inserted into the fish registers 140ºF/60ºC. Depending on the thickness of the cut, this should take 5 to 6 minutes.

While the salmon is cooking, heat the pea sauce slowly over medium-low heat, stirring occasionally, until it starts to bubble. Remove from the heat and set aside until the salmon is done.

Divide the pea sauce equally among 4 plates, and place the salmon on top. Serve immediately.

MOLLY'S TOFU TACOS

MAKES 6 TACOS

MOLLY DWYER, THE UBER-TALENTED CHEF DE CUISINE AT ANDY'S RESTAURANT, TREMONT 647, CREATED THIS FABULOUS VEGETARIAN DISH. THE GOAL FOR TREMONT 647 VEGETARIAN OPTIONS IS THAT THEY'RE SO GOOD EVERYONE WANTS TO ORDER THEM. AND THESE DEFINITELY ACHIEVE THE GOAL. SURE, WE LOVE PORK IN OUR TACOS, BUT WITH THE ZINGY CITRUS AND FRESH, SOUTHEAST ASIAN–INSPIRED FLAVORS, THESE ARE SO SATISFYING THAT EVEN THE MOST DEVOTED CARNIVORES WON'T FEEL THEY'RE MISSING ANYTHING.

IT'S BEST TO GRILL THE TOFU OVER A MEDIUM OR LOW CHARCOAL FIRE. THE MARINADE HAS SESAME OIL IN IT AND CAN FLARE UP IF THE HEAT IS TOO HIGH, WHICH WOULD MAKE THE TOFU BITTER.

¾ cup/180g sambal (chili garlic paste)

½ cup/120ml tamari or soy sauce

½ cup/120ml fresh lime juice

¼ cup/60ml sesame oil

1 tbsp/15ml agave syrup or honey

12 oz/340g piece firm tofu, cut into thirds

6 (5"/13cm) corn or flour tortillas

Sriracha Aioli, for serving (recipe follows)

1 carrot, peeled and shredded

1 cup/120g peeled and shredded daikon radish

10 leaves Thai basil, roughly chopped (or half basil and half cilantro)

10 mint leaves, roughly chopped

In a small bowl, whisk together the sambal, tamari, lime juice, sesame oil and agave. Place the tofu in a flat-bottomed bowl and pour the marinade over it. Cover and refrigerate for 24 to 48 hours.

Build a medium direct fire. Spread an even layer of unlit charcoal in the bottom of the grill. Fill a chimney halfway with charcoal. Stuff two sheets of newspaper in the bottom of the chimney and light it. When the coals are fully engaged—you should see flames peeking over the top—pour them over the unlit charcoal. If using a gas grill, turn the gas on and adjust the temperature on both sides to medium.

When you can hold your hands over the fire for no more than 5 to 8 seconds, clean the grill grate. Remove the tofu from the marinade and grill for 3 minutes, until golden. Flip the tofu and grill for another 3 minutes, until the other side is golden and the tofu is warm throughout.

Remove the tofu from the grill and cut each piece into ½-inch/13mm-thick slices. Set the tortillas on the grill for 30 seconds each, to toast slightly.

Arrange the tortillas on plates, spread about 1 tablespoon/15ml of Sriracha Aioli in the center of each, and evenly divide the tofu. Sprinkle with the carrot and daikon, drizzle with aioli, then garnish with the fresh herbs. Serve immediately.

SRIRACHA AIOLI

OKAY, WE CHEAT A LITTLE BIT HERE, BUT WE JUST LOVE KEWPIE MAYONNAISE, WHICH YOU CAN FIND IN MOST ASIAN MARKETS. IT HAS A TANG AND CREAMINESS THAT YOU CAN'T GET ANYWHERE ELSE. YOU CAN ALSO SUBSTITUTE YOUR FAVORITE MAYO.

1 cup/240ml Kewpie mayonnaise

¼ cup/60ml Sriracha (or your favorite Asian hot sauce)

½ tsp ground white pepper

In a small bowl, whisk together the Kewpie mayo, Sriracha and white pepper. Cover and refrigerate for up to 1 week.

GRILLED ZUCCHINI SALAD WITH SEA SALT AND LEMON ZEST

MAKES 4 SIDE-DISH SERVINGS

THERE'S A REAL SKILL TO PERFECTLY GRILLING ZUCCHINI, EGGPLANT AND SUMMER SQUASH—A SECOND TOO LONG AND YOU HAVE A MUSHY PIECE OF WE DON'T KNOW WHAT. THE KEY IS TO REMEMBER THAT, JUST LIKE A STEAK OR PIECE OF FISH, VEGETABLES KEEP COOKING AFTER THEY ARE REMOVED FROM THE HEAT SOURCE. SO IT'S IMPORTANT TO GET THEM OFF THE FIRE EARLY ENOUGH.

MAKE SURE NOT TO OVER-OIL VEGETABLES BEFORE YOU GRILL THEM. ZUCCHINI ABSORBS OIL, AND TOO MUCH WOULD MAKE THE SALAD GREASY OR THE OIL COULD DRIP AND CAUSE A FLARE-UP. WHEN YOU HAVE A FLARE-UP, SOOT, OR CARBON, ENVELOPS THE FOOD, LEAVING A BITTER TASTE IN YOUR MOUTH.

2 tbsp/30ml olive oil

2 medium-size zucchini, ends removed, sliced lengthwise ½"/13mm thick

Kosher salt and freshly cracked black pepper, to taste

Juice of 2 lemons

2 tbsp/20g slivered almonds, toasted

2 tbsp/10g roughly chopped parsley

5 basil leaves, roughly chopped

4 mint leaves, roughly chopped

1 tbsp/15ml grated Parmesan cheese

Coarse sea salt, for serving

Build a medium direct fire. Spread an even layer of unlit charcoal in the bottom of the grill. Fill a chimney halfway with charcoal. Stuff two sheets of newspaper in the bottom of the chimney and light it. When the coals are fully engaged—you should see flames peeking over the top—pour them over the unlit charcoal. If using a gas grill, light the gas and adjust the temperature on both sides to medium.

Lightly oil the zucchini and season with salt and pepper.

When you can hold your hands over the fire for no more than 5 to 8 seconds, clean the grill grate. Place the zucchini on the grill and cook for 2 to 3 minutes. Flip and cook for 2 to 3 minutes more, until it is golden brown and the zucchini is firm but you can bend it with tongs. Remove from the heat and place on a cutting board.

Slice the zucchini crosswise about ¼ inch/6mm thick and place in a bowl. Add the remaining ingredients to the zucchini and toss very gently to combine. Sprinkle sea salt over the salad and serve immediately or set aside at room temperature until serving time.

HONEY-GRILLED HOT PEPPER JELLY

MAKES 1 QUART/946ML

THIS JELLY IS DELICIOUS ON CRACKERS WITH A NICE TRIPLE-CREAM CHEESE. OR YOU CAN SPREAD IT ON PORK CHOPS TO GIVE THEM AN AWESOME KICK. FEEL FREE TO CHANGE THE PEPPERS TO ACHIEVE DIFFERENT LEVELS OF HEAT.

WHEN WE GRILL PEPPERS, IT IS ONE OF THE FEW TIMES WE ARE ACTUALLY TRYING TO BURN SOMETHING, THOUGH WE CALL IT CHARRING (A LITTLE LESS ARSON/A LITTLE MORE CULINARY). YOU HAVE TO WATCH THEM CAREFULLY BECAUSE THE OBJECTIVE IS TO CHAR THE SKIN WHILE KEEPING THE FLESH INTACT.

---

1 red bell pepper

1 green bell pepper

1 yellow bell pepper

2 jalapeño peppers

1 serrano pepper

2 cups/400g sugar mixed with 1 oz/28g powdered apple pectin or 1 (1.75-oz/50g) package citrus pectin

½ cup/120ml red wine vinegar

½ cup/120ml honey

2 tsp/4g minced rosemary leaves

1 tsp toasted and ground cumin seed

Build a medium direct fire. Spread an even layer of unlit charcoal in the bottom of the grill. Fill a chimney halfway with charcoal. Stuff two sheets of newspaper in the bottom of the chimney and light it. When the coals are fully engaged—you should see flames peeking over the top—pour them over the unlit charcoal. If using a gas grill, light the gas and adjust the temperature on both sides to medium.

When you can hold your hands over the fire for no more than 5 to 8 seconds, clean the grill grate. Place the peppers on the grill; you may have to do this in stages, depending on how big your grill is. Using tongs, as the peppers start to char, turn them over to get the entire surface area exposed to the fire. The peppers should be about 70 percent charred or black, which will take 3 to 5 minutes. Transfer the peppers to a stainless steel bowl and cover tightly with plastic wrap. Let sit for 10 minutes to steam and loosen the skins.

Working with one pepper at a time, rub the charred skin off with your fingers, and remove the stem, core and seeds.

Cut the peppers into ¼ inch/6mm dice. Place in a bowl and set aside.

In a medium-size saucepan, combine the sugar with pectin, vinegar, honey, rosemary and cumin over medium-high heat, whisking until the sugar dissolves. Add the chopped peppers and increase the heat to high. Bring to a rolling boil, stirring, and boil for 1 minute. Remove from the heat. Allow to cool completely, then place in your favorite jelly jars.

ROASTING FOR FLAVOR
APPETIZERS

TUNA CARPACCIO WITH GRILLED VEGETABLE VINAIGRETTE

THIS IS A PERFECT LIGHT SUMMER APPETIZER FOR A SMALL PARTY. YOU CAN MAKE THE VINAIGRETTE IN ADVANCE AND THE TUNA THE DAY YOU WILL BE SERVING IT. THERE WILL BE PLENTY OF VINAIGRETTE LEFT OVER, AND IT'S DELICIOUS ON LOCAL GREENS OR SLICED CUCUMBERS.

WHEN YOU'RE MAKING CARPACCIO, WHETHER IT'S MEAT OR FISH, IT IS IMPORTANT FOR THE FINAL PRODUCT TO BE EVEN AND THIN. THIS TAKES PRACTICE—LOTS OF FUN AND TASTY PRACTICE.

1 small zucchini, ends removed, cut lengthwise into ½"/13mm-thick slices

1 red onion, cut into ½"/13mm-thick slices

1 red bell pepper, cored, seeded and sliced vertically

1 yellow bell pepper, cored, seeded and sliced vertically

Olive oil, for brushing

Kosher salt and freshly ground black pepper, to taste

8 basil leaves, roughly chopped

1 small clove garlic, minced

1 tbsp/15ml olive oil

Juice and zest of 1 lemon

4 oz/113g sushi-quality tuna, cut into four 1 oz/28g pieces

Black pepper, to taste

Equipment: Baking sheet, wooden spoon, 4 refrigerated round plates (at least 6"/15cm in diameter)

Build a medium direct fire. Spread an even layer of unlit charcoal in the bottom of the grill. Fill a chimney halfway with charcoal. Stuff two sheets of newspaper in the bottom of the chimney and light it. When the coals are fully engaged—you should see flames peeking over the top—pour them over the unlit charcoal. If using a gas grill, light the gas and adjust the temperature on both sides to medium.

While the grill is heating, spread the zucchini, onion and peppers on a baking sheet, lightly brush with the olive oil, and season with salt and pepper.

When you can hold your hands over the fire for no more than 5 to 8 seconds, clean the grill grate. Set the vegetables on the grate and grill for 2 to 3 minutes, until they are just starting to brown. Using a pair of tongs or a spatula, carefully rotate the vegetables 45 degrees and cook for 2 more minutes. Flip them and grill for another 2 minutes, then remove from the heat and let cool to room temperature.

Once the vegetables have cooled, dice them into ¼ inch/6mm squares and set them in a small mixing bowl. Add the basil, garlic, olive oil and lemon juice and zest, and toss. Season with salt and pepper to taste. Refrigerate until ready to use.

(continued)

Now comes the fun part. Lay a piece of plastic wrap about the size of a dinner plate on a cutting board. Place a piece of tuna in the middle and set a second piece of plastic wrap, the same size as the first, on top. With the back of a wooden spoon, slowly pound the tuna, using medium-hard strokes, until it is uniformly paper-thin. A 1 ounce/28g piece should end up flat and about 3 to 4 inches/7 to 10cm in diameter. Remove the top piece of plastic wrap, carefully slide your hand under the tuna and turn it over onto the cold plate. Cover the plate tightly with plastic wrap and refrigerate until you are ready to serve, preferably at least 4 hours. Repeat with the remaining pieces.

About a half hour before serving, remove the vinaigrette from the refrigerator. When it comes to room temperature, stir and re-season if necessary.

To serve, remove the plastic wrap from the tuna. Using a slotted spoon, remove about 2 tablespoons/30g of the vegetables from the vinaigrette and mound in the center of a piece of tuna. Repeat with each piece of tuna. Drizzle about 2 teaspoons/10ml of the vinaigrette around each vegetable mound. Grind fresh black pepper over the tuna and serve immediately.

ROGER'S OLYMPIA BARBECUE OYSTERS

ANDY'S FATHER, ROGER, USED TO GRILL OLYMPIA OYSTERS WITH BARBECUE SAUCE FOR SPECIAL OCCASIONS. WE TRIED THEM, LOVED THEM AND HAD TO PUT THEM IN THE BOOK. THANKS, ROGER.

GRILLING OYSTERS CAN BE DIFFICULT, BECAUSE THE BEST WAY TO GRILL THEM IS CUP-SIDE DOWN, BUT THAT WAY THEY CAN WOBBLE. TO HOLD THEM STEADY, WE ROLL RECTANGLES OF ALUMINUM FOIL INTO ½-INCH/13MM-THICK (OR SO) "POLES" THAT WE LAY ALONG THE GRILL GRATES. WE SPACE THEM RELATIVELY CLOSE TOGETHER AND SET THE OYSTERS BETWEEN, WITH THEIR BOTTOMS JUST GRAZING THE GRATES BUT SECURE ENOUGH THAT WE DON'T HAVE TO WORRY THAT THEY WILL SPILL THEIR JUICES.

2 tbsp/30g butter

2 tbsp/30ml olive oil

1 large clove garlic, minced

¼ cup/60ml ketchup

Juice and zest of 1 lemon

1 tbsp/5g minced fresh horseradish

1 tbsp/15ml Sriracha or any hot Asian chili sauce

1 tbsp/15ml rice wine vinegar

2 tsp/8g brown sugar

2 tsp/10ml Worcestershire sauce

½ tsp kosher salt

24 of your favorite oysters

Equipment: Aluminum foil (optional)

Make the barbecue sauce: In a small saucepan over medium-low heat, stir the butter, olive oil and garlic until the butter has melted but not browned and the garlic is fragrant, 2 to 3 minutes. Remove from the heat and stir in the rest of the ingredients, except the oysters, mixing until well combined. Set aside until ready to use.

Build a medium direct fire. Spread an even layer of unlit charcoal in the bottom of the grill. Fill a chimney halfway with charcoal. Stuff two sheets of newspaper in the bottom of the chimney and light it. When the coals are fully engaged—you should see flames peeking over the top—pour them over the unlit charcoal. If using a gas grill, light the gas and adjust the temperature on both sides to medium.

When you can hold your hands over the fire for no more than 5 to 8 seconds, clean the grill grate. Set out the foil "poles," if using. Place the oysters flat side up on the grill. (For 24 oysters we suggest working in two batches.) Cover the grill and cook for 2 to 4 minutes, checking after 2 minutes to see if the oysters have started to open. Once they have opened about ¼ inch/6mm, use tongs to transfer them to a plate or foil pan, being careful not to spill any of their liquor.

Using heatproof gloves, remove the flat top shell and loosen the oyster with an oyster or paring knife, leaving it in the shell with the juices. Add about 1 teaspoon of the barbecue sauce to each oyster and place them back on the grill. Cover the grill and cook for 2 minutes more, until the sauce is hot and bubbly. Serve immediately.

WOOD-ROASTED PORK TENDERLOIN WITH GRILLED BRUSCHETTA AND PORK BUTTER SPREAD

MAKES 4 TO 6 APPETIZER SERVINGS

YES, WE KNOW—PORK BUTTER. PRETTY COOL, RIGHT? YOU'LL DEFINITELY TURN SOME HEADS WITH THIS RECIPE. IN A GOOD WAY. THE IDEA WITH THIS RECIPE IS TO CREATE A CHARCUTERIE-STYLE DISH WITHOUT THE LONG CURE TIMES OR OTHER COMPLEX ELEMENTS OF THAT CRAFT. THE PORK BUTTER, WHICH IS OUR SHORTCUT VERSION OF PORK PÂTÉ OR RILLETTES, KEEPS FOR A WHILE, SO YOU CAN MAKE IT SEVERAL DAYS BEFORE THE REST OF THE DISH.

THE FIRST THING TO KNOW HERE IS THAT THE PORK TENDERLOIN, A WONDERFUL CUT FROM THE HOG, IS TENDER, FULL OF FLAVOR AND LOW IN FAT. WHEN MEATS ARE LOW IN FAT, COOKING THEM TO THE RIGHT TEMPERATURE IS EXTREMELY IMPORTANT. UNLIKE BEEF, RARE PORK IS NOT GOING TO FLY; ON THE OTHER HAND, WELL-DONE PORK IS DRY AND USELESS. PROFESSIONAL COOKS WORK WITH TOUCH AND FEEL TO KNOW WHEN MEAT IS READY (PORK SHOULD BE FIRM WITH A SLIGHT GIVE). UNTIL YOU MASTER THE TOUCH—WHICH WE ARE CONFIDENT YOU WILL DO—WE STRONGLY SUGGEST YOU MONITOR THE TEMPERATURE WITH A THERMOMETER.

1 pork tenderloin, approximately 1½ lb/680g

2 tbsp/35g sea salt

2 tbsp/10g Salt-Free Charcuterie-Style Rub (recipe follows)

12 slices crusty baguette

2 cloves garlic

High-quality olive oil, for drizzling

1 cup/240ml Pork Butter Spread (recipe follows)

Finishing salt, such as smoked, flavored or grey sea salt

Rub the pork all over with sea salt. Place on a baking sheet, cover and refrigerate overnight.

Build a medium direct fire. Spread an even layer of charcoal in the bottom of the grill. Fill a chimney halfway with charcoal. Stuff newspaper in the bottom of the chimney and light it. When the coals are fully engaged—you should see flames peeking over the top—pour them over the unlit charcoal. If using a gas grill, light the gas and adjust the temperature on both sides to medium.

(continued)

Remove the pork from the refrigerator. Transfer to a platter lined with paper towels. Dry the pork and sprinkle with the rub.

When you can hold your hands over the fire for no more than 5 to 8 seconds, clean the grill grate. Place the pork on the grill and cook about 3 minutes per side on all sides, 12 to 14 minutes total, until the internal temperature reaches 140ºF/60ºC. Transfer the pork to a plate and let rest at room temperature for 30 minutes. Either proceed with the recipe or wrap the pork tightly in plastic wrap and refrigerate until ready to use. The pork can be refrigerated for up to 2 days. If it has been refrigerated, let it sit at room temperature for 1 hour before continuing.

Make the bruschetta: Let the fire cool down for about 15 minutes to low heat, or build a low direct fire. (Follow the directions above but fill the chimney one-third full with charcoal and wait until you can hold your hands over the fire for 8 to 10 seconds.) Grill the bread on both sides until lightly toasted, about 1 minute per side. Rub each slice of toasted baguette with the garlic and drizzle with the olive oil.

Slice the pork into ½ inch/13mm-thick slices. Smear each piece of grilled bread with a generous portion of soft pork butter. Place a slice of pork on top and sprinkle with a scant bit of finishing salt. Arrange on a platter and serve.

SALT-FREE CHARCUTERIE-STYLE RUB

MAKES ¼ CUP/20G

1 tbsp/5g fennel seed, coarsely ground in a spice grinder

1 tbsp/5g garlic powder

½ tbsp/2.5g onion powder

½ tbsp/2.5g paprika

1 tsp crushed red pepper flakes

1 tsp ground coriander

1 tsp freshly ground black pepper

In a small bowl, mix all the ingredients until blended. Cover and reserve. The rub will keep, covered, in a cool place for up to 1 month.

PORK BUTTER SPREAD

2 lb/907g pork shoulder, cut into 2" to 3"/5 to 8cm chunks

Kosher salt and freshly cracked black pepper, to taste

1 cup/240ml chicken broth

1 medium carrot, peeled and thinly sliced

1 medium onion, chopped

¼ cup/20g chopped fresh sage leaves, plus ½ tbsp/2.5g minced

1 cup/227g salted butter (preferably European style)

Equipment: Cast-iron pot with lid

Prepare the grill for hot two-zone grilling. Pile unlit charcoals on one side of the grill. Fill a chimney with charcoal. Stuff two sheets of newspaper in the bottom of the chimney and light it. When the coals are fully engaged—you should see flames peeking over the top—pour them over the unlit charcoal. Cover the grill and open the vents all the way. If using a gas grill, light the gas and turn on just one side to high.

Season the pork with salt and pepper. When the temperature of the fire reaches 350ºF/177ºC, clean the grill grate. Grill the pork directly over the fire, turning, until well charred on all sides, about 15 minutes total. Transfer the pork to a cast-iron pot with a lid. Add the broth, carrot and onion and cover. Set the pot on the grill directly over the coals and bring to a boil. Move the pot to the cool side of the grill and cook for 3 hours. (You can also braise the meat in a 350ºF/177ºC oven for 3 hours.)

After 3 hours, test the meat with a fork. It should be very tender and the fork should glide in with little resistance. Remove the pot from the grill and add the chopped sage. Let sit at room temperature, uncovered, for 1 hour. Remove the butter from the refrigerator to soften.

Transfer the pork chunks to a blender or food processor with ¼ cup/60ml of the braising liquid. Pulse until the pork just starts reaching a pasty consistency. Avoid overprocessing; it's okay to have some strands or chunks.

Place the butter in a bowl. Fold in the pork mixture and minced sage. Spoon the pork butter into a crock and refrigerate, covered, or roll it in parchment paper, wrap tightly in plastic wrap and freeze. It will keep for 1 week in the refrigerator, 2 months in the freezer.

BEEF AND ASPARAGUS ROULADE WITH SESAME AND SCALLIONS

SERVES 4 AS AN APPETIZER

THIS DISH IS A PERFECT APPETIZER FOR A SMALL DINNER PARTY. THE GOAL OF THE RECIPE IS TO COOK THE MEAT EVENLY AND SLIGHTLY WARM THE ASPARAGUS. IT TAKES SOME SKILL WITH TONGS AND FIRE TEMPERATURE, BUT IT'S A GREAT DISH TO PRACTICE TECHNIQUE. AND THE REWARD IS YUMMY.

TOGARASHI IS THE JAPANESE WORD FOR RED CHILE PEPPER. IN THE UNITED STATES, SOME TOGARASHI BLENDS ARE A MIX OF CHILE PEPPERS, SESAME SEEDS, SEAWEED AND OTHER INGREDIENTS. THEY CAN RANGE FROM MILD TO EXTREMELY HOT. WE LIKE OURS HOT.

---

8 oz/224g beef tenderloin

1 small shallot, minced

2 scallions, cut into ⅛"/3mm rings, divided

1 tbsp/15ml Dijon mustard

1 tbsp/15ml agave nectar or honey

1 tbsp/15ml tamari or soy sauce

1 tbsp/5g toasted sesame seeds, divided

2 tsp/10ml rice wine vinegar

8 asparagus spears, blanched to al dente

Vegetable oil, for cooking

Kosher salt and freshly ground black pepper, to taste

Togarashi, for garnish

Equipment: Toothpicks

Build a medium direct fire. Spread an even layer of unlit charcoal in the bottom of the grill. Fill a chimney halfway with charcoal. Stuff two sheets of newspaper in the bottom of the chimney and light it. When the coals are fully engaged—you should see flames peeking over the top—pour them over the unlit charcoal. If you are using a gas grill, light the gas and adjust the temperature on both sides to medium.

Slice the beef against the grain into 4 equal rounds, about 2 ounces/56g each. Lay the meat flat and pound lightly with the back of a spoon to about ¼ inch/6mm thickness.

In a small bowl, mix the shallot, half the scallions, mustard, agave, tamari, half the sesame seeds and vinegar. Lay the beef slices on a plate and brush them generously with the shallot mixture. Place 2 asparagus spears on the left side of each piece of meat. Beginning at the asparagus end, start rolling, until you have a roll-up. Fasten with toothpicks. Repeat with the remaining beef slices and asparagus spears.

When you can hold your hands over the fire for no more than 5 to 8 seconds, clean the grill grate. Lightly brush vegetable oil on the outside of the rolls and season with salt and pepper. Place on the grill and sear for 45 seconds to 1 minute, until a crust starts to develop. Roll, and repeat for about 5 to 7 minutes, until all sides are seared and there is an internal temperature of 130ºF/54ºC.

Transfer the roulades to a wire rack and brush with the remaining sauce; allow to rest for 5 minutes. To serve, sprinkle with the remaining sesame seeds, the remaining scallions and the togarashi. And have a glass of sake.

CHAPTER 3

AVOID THE BURN: LOW DIRECT GRILLING

Low direct grilling, a technique in which food is grilled directly over a low fire, is perfect when you want to slowly develop an exterior sear, or crust, while cooking the food all the way through. The standard test for a low fire is holding your hand over the flame. You want to be able to hold it there for about 8 to 10 seconds. This technique is perfect for a dish like the Slow-Grilled Chicken Thighs (page 85), which develop a crispy exterior and juicy, tender meat. John and Andrea's Grilled Narragansett Pizza (page 87) is another recipe that was made for a low direct grill, because you want the pizza crust to be crunchy when you bite into it, yet have a nice, soft chew. Trying to make this over a fire that's too hot would give you pizza crackers—which might not be bad, but definitely not what we're after.

SLOW-GRILLED CHICKEN THIGHS WITH ALABAMA WHITE SAUCE

MAKES 4 TO 6 SERVINGS

THE BEAUTY OF THIS RECIPE IS CRISPY, GOLDEN BROWN SKIN, ACHIEVED BY COATING THE CHICKEN PIECES WITH DRY RUB BEFORE GRILLING—AND A LITTLE BIT OF TECHNIQUE. BY COOKING THE CHICKEN OVER LOW, DIRECT HEAT YOU VASTLY REDUCE THE RISK OF BURNING THE SKIN. WHEN USING CHARCOAL, IT'S IMPORTANT TO WATCH OUT FOR HOT SPOTS. IF THEY OCCUR, SIMPLY MOVE THE CHICKEN TO A COOLER PART OF THE GRILL.

ALABAMA WHITE SAUCE (AKA ALABAMA WHITE BBQ SAUCE OR JUST PLAIN WHITE BBQ SAUCE) IS A REGIONAL ODDITY THAT IS VIRTUALLY UNKNOWN OUTSIDE OF NORTHERN ALABAMA. TANGY AND RICH, WITH A KICK OF HORSERADISH, IT IS TYPICALLY PAIRED WITH CHICKEN BUT TASTES GREAT WITH JUST ABOUT ANYTHING YOU CAN THINK TO POUR IT ON OR DIP IN IT.

1 tbsp/18g kosher salt

1 tbsp/12g turbinado sugar

1 tbsp/5g smoked or sweet paprika

2 tsp/4g coarsely ground black pepper

1 tsp garlic powder

½ tsp cayenne

8 bone-in, skin-on chicken thighs, about 4 oz/113g each

Alabama White Sauce (recipe follows)

Make the dry rub: In a small bowl, mix all the seasonings. Set aside.

Build a low direct fire. Spread an even layer of unlit charcoal in the bottom of the grill. Fill a chimney one-third full with charcoal. Stuff two sheets of newspaper in the bottom of the chimney and light it. When the coals are fully engaged—you should see flames peeking over the top—pour them over the unlit charcoal. If using a gas grill, light the gas and adjust the temperature on both sides to low.

While the fire is coming to temperature, place the chicken thighs on a baking sheet, skin-side up. Sprinkle the chicken with half of the dry rub.

When you can hold your hands over the fire for no more than 8 to 10 seconds, clean the grill grate. Set the chicken thighs, skin-side down, on the grates. Sprinkle the remaining half of the dry rub on the chicken. Cook, covered, for 30 to 40 minutes, checking periodically to avoid excessive charring on the skin. Rotate thighs over the fire if there are hot spots. If using a charcoal grill, adjust the vents to maintain a temperature of 300ºF/149ºC.

Flip the chicken and continue to cook until a thermometer inserted into the thickest part of the meat registers 170ºF/77ºC, about 15 to 20 minutes more. Transfer the chicken to a platter and let it rest for 10 minutes. Slather with the Alabama White Sauce and serve.

ALABAMA WHITE SAUCE

1 cup/240g mayonnaise (we prefer Kewpie)

½ cup/120ml apple cider vinegar

¼ cup/60ml light corn syrup

1 tbsp/15ml prepared horseradish

1 tbsp/15ml fresh lemon juice

1 tsp salt

1 tsp pepper

1 tsp cayenne pepper sauce (or your favorite hot sauce)

Whisk all the ingredients in a medium-size mixing bowl until fully incorporated. Cover and set aside until ready to use, or transfer to an airtight jar and refrigerate for up to 2 weeks.

JOHN AND ANDREA'S GRILLED NARRAGANSETT PIZZA

OUR FRIENDS, JOHN AND ANDREA, INVITE US TO THEIR SUMMER HOME IN NARRAGANSETT, RHODE ISLAND, NOW AND THEN (WE'RE A LOT TO HANDLE). WHEN THEY FIRST TOLD US THEY WERE GOING TO MAKE GRILLED PIZZA, WE HAD NO IDEA HOW FANTASTIC IT WOULD BE. THE KEY IS A LOW, EVENLY SPREAD FIRE AND GETTING THE DOUGH EVEN. ANDREA'S TRICK OF STRETCHING IT ON THE BACK OF A COOKIE SHEET WORKS BEAUTIFULLY. NOW IF ONLY THEY WERE AS GOOD IN FANTASY FOOTBALL . . .

GRILLING PIZZA IS AN ADVANCED SPORT. IT DEFINITELY TAKES JUST THE RIGHT TOUCH. YOU MIGHT WANT TO MAKE SOME EXTRA DOUGH AND PRACTICE (OR, YES, YOU CAN BUY IT FROZEN). WHEN IT'S DONE RIGHT, GRILLED DOUGH IS AS GOOD AS IT GETS. IF IT'S OVERCOOKED OR BURNED IN AN AREA, JUST BREAK THAT PIECE OFF AND BRUSH THE REST WITH EXTRA VIRGIN OLIVE OIL AND A LITTLE PARMESAN, AND IT'S GOOD TO EAT.

¾ cup/180ml warm tap water, 120°F/48°C

½ cup/120ml apple juice, at room temperature

1 tsp active dry yeast

1 clove garlic, minced

2 tsp/10ml extra-virgin olive oil, plus more for bowls and shaping pizza dough

1½ tsp/6g sugar

1 tsp honey

2 tsp/4g minced fresh rosemary

3 cups/360g all-purpose flour

1½ tsp/9g kosher salt

1 tsp ground black pepper

3 cups/480g Caramelized Onions (recipe follows)

3 cups/480g pickled Italian hot peppers, strained

3 cups/450g bacon, cooked until crisp, roughly chopped (about 10 slices)

1 cup/120g crumbled blue cheese, such as Great Hill or Bayley Hazen

1½ cups/225g grated mozzarella

1 cup/60g fresh basil, minced (about ⅓ cup/20g per pizza)

Equipment: Food thermometer, 3 baking sheets

(continued)

In a medium-size glass bowl, combine the water and apple juice. It should be warm to the touch, about 105°F/41°C. (If necessary, you can microwave for 10 to 20 seconds to warm it.) Stir in the yeast and let sit until it bubbles, about 5 minutes. Add the garlic, 2 tsp/10ml olive oil, sugar, honey and rosemary, and mix well with a fork.

In the bowl of a stand mixer fitted with a dough hook (or in a large bowl, using your hands), combine the flour, salt and pepper. Add the yeast mixture, and blend on medium speed until the flour is thoroughly moistened and the dough starts to pull away from the sides of the bowl, 3 to 5 minutes. Increase the speed to medium-high and beat until elastic and smooth, 7 to 10 minutes (or turn out onto a floured surface and knead vigorously by hand for 12 to 15 minutes).

Coat a large, clean bowl with olive oil. Shape the dough into a ball and place in the oiled bowl, rotating to coat. Cover with a barely damp cloth and let rest in a warm place until doubled in size, 1 to 2 hours.

Transfer the dough to a clean surface. Punch it down and divide into thirds, rolling each piece so all 3 are perfect balls.

Place the balls in a large, oiled bowl, cover with a towel and leave at room temperature until doubled in size, about 30 to 40 minutes.

Build a low direct fire. Spread an even layer of unlit charcoal in the bottom of the grill. Fill a chimney one-third full with charcoal. Stuff two sheets of newspaper in the bottom of the chimney and light it. When the coals are fully engaged—you should see flames peeking over the top—pour them over the unlit charcoal. If you are using a gas grill, light the gas and turn both sides to low.

While the fire is heating up, place a dough ball on the back of a baking sheet. Using your palms, evenly push down on the dough to make into a disk. Use consistent pressure, push and stretch the dough repeatedly until it is an even ¼ inch/6mm thick. Turn the disk over, brush a little more oil on the top and bottom and continue the process until it is ⅛ inch/3mm thick all around and roughly 10 inches/25 cm in diameter. Bonus point if it's in a perfect circle, but it's okay if it's not; it'll still taste yummy.

Repeat the process for each dough ball.

When you can hold your hands over the fire for no more than 8 to 10 seconds, clean the grill grate and set all of your toppings next to the grill. The rest of the process goes pretty quickly.

Working quickly, take one pizza round from a baking sheet and lay it flat on the grate. Let it cook until it is light golden brown and easily pulls away from the grate, about 2 to 4 minutes. Turn it over and quickly and evenly spread the onions, peppers, bacon and cheeses over the dough. Cover the grill and cook the pizza for 2 to 4 minutes, until the bottom of the crust is golden brown and the cheese has started to melt.

Using two spatulas, carefully transfer the pizza to a cutting board. Cut into 3-inch/8cm squares (our favorite way) or 6 to 8 slices. Garnish with the freshly chopped basil and serve immediately.

Cook your next pizza quickly, because the last one is gone.

CARAMELIZED ONIONS

MAKES 3 CUPS/480G

2 tbsp/30ml olive oil

2 large sweet onions, sliced

1 tsp salt

Heat the vegetable oil in a heavy-bottomed sauté pan or cast-iron skillet over medium heat. Add the onions and salt and cook, stirring frequently, for 10 to 15 minutes, or until the onions soften and turn golden brown. Remove from the heat and cool to room temperature.

GRILLED TROUT STUFFED WITH FRESH HERB SALAD

MAKES 4 SERVINGS

TROUT IS THIN AND DELICATE AND COOKS QUICKLY, SO GRILLING IT IS QUITE A CHALLENGE. BUT THE REWARD IS IMMENSE, AS FRESH TROUT IS SWEET AND FLAKY AND REALLY PICKS UP THE GRILL'S SMOKY FLAVORS. AND THE SKIN, WHICH IS EDIBLE, BECOMES DELICIOUSLY CRISPY. WE SUGGEST THROWING SOME SOAKED FRUIT WOOD CHIPS, SUCH AS APPLE OR CHERRY, ON THE FIRE JUST BEFORE YOU START COOKING.

IT'S REALLY IMPORTANT TO HAVE A LOW, EVEN FIRE, A REALLY CLEAN GRILL AND TWO SPATULAS.

1 cup/80g packed arugula leaves

1 shallot, julienned

¼ cup/16g lightly packed parsley leaves

6 large basil leaves, torn into 4 pieces each

2 sprigs tarragon

1 tbsp/5g roughly chopped fresh dill

Juice and minced zest of 1 Meyer lemon, about 1 tbsp/15ml (if you can't find Meyer, a regular lemon is okay)

1½ tsp/7.5ml olive oil

Kosher salt and freshly ground black pepper, to taste

Vegetable oil, for grilling

4 (12-oz/340g) boneless trout, preferably with heads on

Equipment: 1 cup/240g fruit wood chips soaked in water for at least 4 hours, 2 flexible fish spatulas (page 93)

Build a low direct fire. Spread an even layer of unlit charcoal in the bottom of the grill. Fill a chimney one-third full with charcoal. Stuff two sheets of newspaper in the bottom of the chimney and light it. When the coals are fully engaged—you should see flames peeking over the top—pour them over the unlit charcoal. The vents should be 75 percent closed, to keep the temperature low. If using a gas grill, light the gas and adjust the temperature on both sides to low.

Toss the arugula, shallot and herbs in a mixing bowl and dress with the lemon juice, zest and olive oil. Season with salt and pepper, and set aside.

Lightly oil the skin of the trout with vegetable oil and season both sides with salt and pepper. Strain the wood chips, and add them to one side of the fire. When you can hold your hands over the fire for no more than 8 to 10 seconds, clean the grill grate. Working with one or two at a time, lay the trout flat, skin-side down, on the side of the grill opposite the wood chips, and cover the grill. Cook for 4 to 6 minutes, until the trout is opaque and firm to the touch. Be very careful not to overcook the fish or it will be hard to maneuver.

(continued)

For gas grills, place the wood chips in a small disposable aluminum pan with tiny holes poked in the bottom and set it over the hot side of the grill. Close the lid and wait 2 to 3 minutes. When you see smoke coming from the grill, lift the lid and lay the trout on the side of the grill opposite the wood chips. Proceed as above.

Now the tricky part: using two spatulas and going with the grate, quickly transfer each trout to a plate. Place a quarter of the salad mixture on one side of the fillet and, using one of the spatulas, fold the other side over the salad. Repeat with each fillet. Eat immediately. This dish is perfect with simple rice.

FISH SPATULAS

Fish spatulas are among our favorite kitchen tools, as valuable outdoors as in. The beauty of a fish spatula is that it is designed to be very pliable. We love them for grilling fish because we can push them hard against the grill grates, then slide them right under the fish. The spatula hugs the grate and simultaneously lifts the fish from the cooking surface. All professional chefs have several of these in their kitchen. You should, too.

AVOID THE BURN
APPETIZERS

DELPHA'S GRILLED CHICKEN WINGS WITH AGAVE AND CREOLE SPICES

MAKES 4 APPETIZER SERVINGS

JOHN DELPHA, WHO OWNS THE BELTED COW BISTRO IN ESSEX JUNCTION, VERMONT, WITH HIS WIFE, KATY, IS ONE OF OUR ALL-TIME FAVORITE CHEFS. TO SAY HE IS A PERFECTIONIST IS AN UNDERSTATEMENT. THUS THESE WINGS TAKE TIME, PRACTICE AND PATIENCE.

IN THIS RECIPE YOU'RE TRYING TO ACHIEVE TWO THINGS—*FULLY COOKED* AND *CRISPY* CHICKEN WINGS. TO DO THIS, YOU NEED A NICE, EVEN, SLOW FIRE. YOU MIGHT HAVE TO PLAY WITH IT A LITTLE TO GET THE TEMPERATURE JUST RIGHT. ONCE YOU'VE MASTERED THIS TECHNIQUE, YOU WILL HAVE NO NEED FOR A FRYER BECAUSE YOU'LL BE ABLE TO SERVE CRISPY WINGS FROM YOUR GRILL ANYTIME.

20 chicken wings, separated into flats and drums

Kosher salt and freshly ground black pepper, to taste

¼ cup/60ml agave nectar

2 tbsp/30ml Creole Spice, or more, to taste (recipe follows)

Tabasco or your favorite hot sauce, for serving

Celery sticks, for serving

Build a low direct fire. Spread an even layer of unlit charcoal in the bottom of the grill. Fill a chimney one-third full with charcoal. Stuff two sheets of newspaper in the bottom of the chimney and light it. When the coals are fully engaged—you should see flames peeking over the top—pour them over the unlit charcoal. If using a gas grill, light the gas and adjust the temperature on both sides to low.

Season the chicken with salt and pepper. When you can hold your hands over the fire for no more than 8 to 10 seconds, clean the grill grate. Place the wings on the grill and cook for about 1 to 2 minutes, then flip the pieces over. Continue cooking, turning the pieces over, for about 10 to 15 minutes, until they are crispy and golden brown, the skin is blistered, and a thermometer inserted into the meat registers 165°F/74°C.

Once the wings are done, transfer them to a large bowl, drizzle with agave and toss to coat completely. Season the wings generously with the Creole Spice and toss again.

Serve immediately with a side of Tabasco and celery sticks.

CREOLE SPICE

2 tbsp/10g dried thyme

2 tbsp/10g dried basil

2 tbsp/10g paprika

2 tsp/12g kosher salt

2 tsp/4g chili powder

2 tsp/4g ground black pepper

1 tsp cayenne pepper

In a small bowl, mix all the ingredients together. Set aside until ready to use. This blend will keep, covered, for up to a month.

AGAVE (AH-GAH-VAY) NECTAR

Agave nectar, or syrup, is made from succulent plants that grow in Mexico, Central America and the American Southwest. The plant is poisonous when raw, but has a mild, sweet flavor—similar to brown sugar—when boiled into syrup. We use agave a lot with grilled food because it makes a delicious sweet-sticky glaze. In sauces, it dissolves more easily than sugar.

THAI-FLAVORED PORK BELLY SKEWERS

MAKES 10 SKEWERS, 4 TO 6 APPETIZER SERVINGS

WE FOUND THAT GRILLING THESE OVER A LOW GRILL HELPS BUILD A WONDERFUL STICKY-CRUNCHY TEXTURE. BE SURE TO FLIP THE SKEWERS OVER EVERY 30 TO 45 SECONDS. SOAKING THE SKEWERS IN WATER HELPS KEEP THEM FROM BURNING.

1 cup/240ml water

½ cup/90g brown sugar

1 stalk lemongrass, thinly sliced

2 pieces star anise

2"/5cm cinnamon stick

2 tsp/4g coriander seeds, toasted and ground

2 tsp/4g red pepper flakes

¼ cup/60ml soy sauce

2 tbsp/30ml fish sauce

2 tbsp/30ml white vinegar

1 lb/450g pork belly, skin removed, cut into 1"/2.5cm square slices, each ¼"/6mm thick

10 scallions, thick white part cut into 1"/2.5cm pieces

Equipment: Ten 8"/20cm wooden skewers, soaked in water for at least 4 hours

In a small saucepan over high heat, bring to a boil the water, brown sugar, lemongrass, star anise, cinnamon stick, coriander and red pepper flakes. Boil for 30 seconds, then remove from the heat and transfer to a bowl. Cover and refrigerate until completely cool, about 2 hours. Add the soy and fish sauces and vinegar and stir.

Place the pork belly chunks in the marinade for at least 4 and up to 24 hours.

Thread the pork belly and scallion alternately onto the skewers, starting with the pork belly (the scallion should be perpendicular to the skewers). Each skewer should have 3 pieces of pork and 2 scallions.

Build a low direct fire. Spread an even layer of unlit charcoal in the bottom of the grill. Fill a chimney one-third full with charcoal. Stuff two sheets of newspaper in the bottom of the chimney and light it. When the coals are fully engaged—you should see flames peeking over the top—pour them over the unlit charcoal. If using a gas grill, light the gas and adjust the temperature on both sides to low.

When you can hold your hands over the fire for no more than 8 to 10 seconds, clean the grill grate. Place the skewers directly over the fire, with the exposed wooden ends pointing to the edge of the grill, and grill for 30 to 45 seconds, until the meat starts to brown. Flip the skewers over and repeat. Continue this process for about 4 minutes, until the meat is dark brown, almost black in some areas.

Serve hot, and make sure you get one for yourself. These will not last long.

CHAPTER 4

GRILLING TWO WAYS: HYBRID TWO-ZONE GRILLING

When we cook outdoors, we utilize the grill as a stove. We use it to perform every kitchen function from sautéing to slow-roasting to, of course, grilling. Beginning in this chapter, we show you how to take advantage of two key grilling techniques—the direct sear you get over charcoal and the ability to use the grill as an oven—and bring them together. This is where the food you produce is the result of more than your ability to follow our recipes. Where your intuition and feel for the fire come into play. Where you really become a grill master, adjusting vents and adding charcoal to maintain a steady grill temperature. In recipes from Grilled Club Steak (page 109) to Laquered Pork Belly (page 132) to Backyard Clambake On Your Grill (page 102), you will be able to apply all the skills we talked about in the beginning of the book. If you're new to grilling, you might want to start at Chapter 1. Don't worry; you'll get here.

BACKYARD CLAMBAKE ON YOUR GRILL

FOR THIS RECIPE, WHICH REPLICATES A CLAMBAKE AT THE BEACH, WE USE THE GRILL IN TWO WAYS: FIRST, AS A DIRECT HEAT SOURCE, AND SECOND, ALMOST AS AN OVEN. MOST SERIOUS GRILLERS DANGLE THE PROBE END OF A REMOTE THERMOMETER THROUGH THE VENT OF THE GRILL COVER. THIS MEASURES THE TEMPERATURE OF THE GRILL ENVIRONMENT BUT NOT THE ACTUAL COOKING SURFACE. WE BELIEVE IT IS MORE USEFUL TO KNOW THE TEMPERATURE WHERE YOU ARE ACTUALLY COOKING THE FOOD, SO WE USE WHAT WE REFER TO AS THE POTATO TRICK. CUT A POTATO IN HALF AND INSERT THE PROBE THROUGH ONE HALF. SET THE POTATO WITH THE PROBE DIRECTLY ON THE GRATE. THE POTATO ANCHORS THE PROBE, SO IT WILL RELAY INFORMATION IN A STEADY FASHION. THIS WAY, YOU KNOW THE TEMPERATURE THROUGHOUT THE COOK TIME.

12 small red potatoes, scrubbed

4 ears corn, shucked and cut in half

1 large sweet onion, cut into quarters

2 links chorizo or linguiça sausage

4 lobster tails, cut in half

2 tbsp/30ml vegetable oil

Kosher salt and freshly ground black pepper, to taste

1 cup/240ml dry white wine

12 littleneck clams, cleaned

12 mussels, cleaned

4 sprigs curly parsley

1 bunch chives, minced, half reserved for garnish

2 tsp/4g Old Bay Seasoning

½ cup/240g unsalted butter

4 sprigs fresh chervil, leaves only, chopped, for garnish

Prepare the grill for hot two-zone grilling. Pile the unlit charcoal on one side of the grill. Fill a chimney with charcoal. Stuff two sheets of newspaper in the bottom of the chimney and light it. When the coals are fully engaged—you should see flames peeking over the top—pour them over the unlit charcoal. Cover the grill and open the vents all the way. If using a gas grill, light the gas and adjust the temperature on one side of the grill to high.

Bring a pot of salted water to a boil on the stove. Add the potatoes and boil for 5 minutes. Add the corn and boil for an additional 3 minutes. Drain. Transfer the potatoes and corn to a 9" x 13"/23 x 33cm aluminum pan and set the pan near the grill.

When the grill temperature reaches 350ºF/177ºC, clean the grate. Grill the onion quarters directly over the fire until charred, about 5 minutes. Transfer to the aluminum pan.

While the onion is cooking, grill the sausages near but not directly over the fire, turning to char all sides, until warmed through, 5 to 8 minutes. Keep the grill covered while cooking the onions and sausage. Transfer the sausages to a cutting board and cut into large chunks. Place in the aluminum pan with the onion, corn and potatoes.

(continued)

Brush the lobster with the vegetable oil and season with salt and pepper. Grill directly over the fire for 3 minutes. Flip and cook for 2 more minutes. Add the lobster to the pan, and pour in the white wine. Set the pan directly over the fire and keep the grill uncovered. When the wine starts to boil, add the clams, mussels, parsley, chives, Old Bay Seasoning and butter, and cover the pan tightly with 2 sheets of heavy-duty aluminum foil.

Slide the pan to the cool side and cover the grill. Leave the vents wide open, making sure the temperature is still at 350°F/177°C. If it shoots up past 375°F/191°C, close the vents a bit to lower the temperature into the target 325°F to 375°F/163°C to 191°C zone. Cover the grill and cook for 20 minutes, or until the mussels and clams have popped open.

Remove the pan from the grill and spoon the shellfish, vegetables and broth into a large serving bowl. Sprinkle with the remaining chives and chervil. Serve immediately with crusty bread to soak up the juices.

BELTED COW BISTRO'S GRILLED PROVOLONE-STUFFED PORK SIRLOIN CHOPS WITH VINEGAR PEPPERS

MAKES 4 SERVINGS

IF YOU'RE NOT CAREFUL, IT CAN BE A LITTLE TOO EASY TO COOK PORK PAST THE POINT OF JUICY TENDERNESS. TO KEEP THE CHOPS IN THIS RECIPE FROM DRYING OUT, WE RECOMMEND A SLIGHT VARIATION ON TWO-ZONE COOKING. START BY SEARING THEM OVER HIGH HEAT, THEN ALMOST FINISH THEM ON THE COOL SIDE OF THE GRILL, AND FINALLY MOVE THEM BACK OVER THE HOT FIRE TO CRISP THE CRUST.

4 pork sirloin chops (bone-in is fine), 7 to 8 oz/198 to 230g each

4 oz/113g provolone, cut into 4 thick slices

Vegetable oil, for rubbing chops

Bacon Salt (recipe follows), to taste

Freshly ground black pepper, to taste

Vinegar Peppers (recipe follows)

Sage leaves, for serving

Prepare the grill for low two-zone grilling. Pile the unlit charcoal on one side of the grill. Fill a chimney with charcoal. Stuff two sheets of newspaper in the bottom of the chimney and light it. When the coals are fully engaged—you should see flames peeking over the top—pour them over the unlit charcoal. Cover the grill and shut the vents 75 percent. If using a gas grill, light the gas and adjust the temperature on one side of the grill to medium.

While the fire is coming to temperature, cut a lengthwise incision into each chop and stuff each with 1 slice of provolone, folded in half. Push the chops closed from the sides and tamp down on top using a wooden spoon so the cheese won't leak out.

Brush the chops lightly on all sides with oil and sprinkle generously with Bacon Salt and pepper. Massage the oil, salt and pepper into the meat to form a paste. Allow to rest for 10 to 15 minutes.

(continued)

When the temperature reaches 250ºF to 300ºF/121ºC to 149ºC, clean the grill grate. When you can hold your hand over the fire no longer than 5 to 8 seconds, place the chops on the grill directly over the fire and sear for about 4 minutes per side. Move to a cooler part of the grill to finish cooking, covered, about 5 minutes, adjusting the vents as necessary to maintain a consistent 225ºF to 300ºF/107ºC to 149ºC. Place the chops over the hot side of the grill to cook, uncovered, for another minute on each side, then transfer to a platter to rest.

While the pork chops are cooking, warm the Vinegar Peppers and some of their pickling liquid in a small saucepan. Place each chop on a warmed plate, drain any juices that have run off of the chops into the peppers and top each chop with some peppers. Garnish with the sage leaves and serve.

BACON SALT

MAKES ½ CUP/120G

¼ cup/72g kosher salt

3 tbsp/36g sugar

2 tbsp/10g hickory smoke powder (see Resources, page 184)

In a small bowl, mix all the ingredients. Will keep, covered, for 3 months.

VINEGAR PEPPERS

MAKES 1 QUART/950ML

¾ cup/180ml white vinegar

¼ cup/60ml red wine vinegar

½ cup/120ml water

1½ tsp/2.5g red pepper flakes

4 red and yellow bell peppers, julienned

In a saucepan over medium heat, bring the vinegars, water and red pepper flakes to a boil. Place the peppers in a bowl. Pour the boiling liquid over the peppers and let stand for at least 15 minutes. Cool. Cover and store in the refrigerator for up to 1 month.

GRILLED CLUB STEAK, HOUSE BUTTER, MONAC'S PILAF

MAKES 2 SERVINGS

THIS RECIPE USES THE REVERSE-SEAR METHOD. FIRST, COOK THE MEAT OVER LOW HEAT TO GET THE INTERIOR DONE RIGHT. THEN RAISE THE FIRE TEMPERATURE AND COOK THE MEAT AGAIN OVER HIGH HEAT, TO GET A GOOD SEAR. THIS IS THE OPPOSITE OF WHAT YOU WOULD TYPICALLY DO ON A KETTLE GRILL. REVERSE SEARING ACHIEVES SIMILAR RESULTS AS TWO-ZONE COOKING THICK CUTS THROUGH WITHOUT BURNING THE EXTERIOR—JUST IN THE OPPOSITE ORDER. IT'S A GREAT METHOD FOR THE BIG GREEN EGG OR OTHER CERAMIC COOKERS, BECAUSE TWO-ZONE COOKING IS NOT REALLY POSSIBLE IN THAT SETUP. CERAMIC COOKERS CAN BE SET UP FOR SLOW COOKING FIRST AND THEN FINISHING HOT. STARTING HOT AND FINISHING COOL CAN BE DIFFICULT, BECAUSE THESE VERY EFFICIENT CERAMIC COOKERS RETAIN HEAT SO WELL.

1½ lb/680g strip loin steak, 3"/ 7.6cm thick

Kosher salt, to taste

4 tbsp/60g House Butter, softened (recipe follows)

Monac's Pilaf (recipe follows)

Equipment: Baking sheet fitted with a wire rack

Cut the meat in half crosswise to create 2 very thick, more or less square steaks. Liberally salt the steaks and let sit at room temperature for 30 to 60 minutes.

Make the House Butter, or remove it from the refrigerator to soften while the steak sits.

Prepare for low two-zone grilling. Pile unlit charcoal on one side of the grill. Fill a chimney with charcoal. Stuff two sheets of newspaper in the bottom of the chimney and light it. When the coals are fully engaged—you should see flames peeking over the top—pour them over the unlit charcoal. Cover the grill and close the vents 75 percent. If using gas, adjust the temperature on one side of the grill to medium.

While you are waiting for the grill to heat up, start the pilaf.

When the temperature reaches 300ºF/149ºC, clean the grill grate. Place the steaks on the cool side of the grill and cover the grill. Cook for 10 minutes, then flip the steaks. Continue cooking on the cool side of the grill, covered, checking the internal temperature of the steak every 3 to 5 minutes, until it reaches 110ºF/43ºC. Transfer the steaks to the baking sheet fitted with a wire rack. The rack prevents the steaks from sitting in potential accumulated juices and getting the surface soggy.

(continued)

Keep the lid off the grill and let the temperature of the fire build. (Or crank the gas grill up to high.) Add more charcoal if necessary. Once the fire is very hot (you should not be able to hold your hands over it for more than 3 to 5 seconds), return the steaks to the grill, placing them directly over the fire this time, and sear them for 2 to 3 minutes per side. At this point the steaks will be rare to medium-rare. If you like them more well done, move them to the cooler side of the grill until they reach an internal temperature of 135ºF/57ºC for medium, 145ºF/63ºC for well done.

Remove the steaks from the grill, and let them rest for 10 minutes. To serve, set on 2 plates and dollop 2 tbsp/30g House Butter on each. Serve with Monac's Pilaf.

HOUSE BUTTER

MAKES ½ CUP/120G

½ cup/120g salted butter, softened

1 tbsp/5g minced parsley

4 cloves roasted garlic, mashed into paste

1 clove garlic, minced

1 tsp Worcestershire sauce

1 tsp finely grated lemon zest

½ tsp finely ground black pepper

Place the butter in a medium bowl. Using a fork, blend in the parsley, both garlics, Worcestershire, lemon zest and pepper. Set aside until the steaks are ready or cover and refrigerate. The butter will keep in the refrigerator for 2 weeks. Or you can roll the butter in wax paper, wrap it in plastic and freeze for 2 months.

MONAC'S PILAF

2 tbsp/30g butter

2 tbsp/30ml olive oil

⅓ cup/80g orzo

1 cup/240g long-grain rice

3 cups/700ml low-sodium chicken broth, heated

Kosher salt and freshly ground black pepper, to taste

1 tbsp/15g crumbled feta

2 tsp/10g minced cured black olives (about 4)

1 tsp chopped parsley

1 tsp julienned mint leaves

In a medium-size saucepan over medium heat, melt the butter with the oil. When the butter is bubbling, add the orzo and toast, stirring, until golden brown. Add the rice and stir for 2 minutes. Add the hot broth and bring to a boil. Stir, cover and reduce the heat to low. Cook until the broth is fully absorbed, about 30 minutes.

Remove from the heat and season with salt and pepper. Fluff the pilaf with a fork. Transfer to a serving bowl and sprinkle with the feta, olives, parsley and mint.

Once the mixture is fragrant, add the bacon, red onion and celery, and continue to cook, stirring, still regulating the temperature by moving the pan to and from coals.

Lightly oil the swordfish steaks and season with salt and pepper. Place on the hot side of the grill and sear for 2 minutes, then rotate 90 degrees to create crosshatch marks. Flip the swordfish and continue to cook until the meat has cooked about one-third of the way up—you can gauge by the color change from translucent to opaque white—and the cooked side is golden brown. Let cook for about 1 minute more, then rotate and cook for another minute. When it's done, the swordfish should be firm with a slight spring to it and have an internal temperature of 140ºF/60ºC. Place the swordfish on a platter or individual plates.

Return the pan with the bacon mixture to the hot side of the grill and, when it sizzles again, add the lobster and lemon juice, stirring until the lobster is warm, about 1 minute, being careful not to burn the butter. If it seems to be getting too hot, move to a cooler part of the grill.

Remove from the heat, season with salt and pepper, and quickly fold in the arugula leaves. Spoon over the swordfish and eat immediately.

GRILLED STRIPER FILLET WITH SUMMER CORN SUCCOTASH

GRILLING FISH FILLETS CAN BE CHALLENGING. UNLIKE TUNA AND SWORDFISH STEAKS, THE FLAKINESS OF COOKED FILLETS MAKES IT HARD TO FLIP AND REMOVE THEM FROM THE GRILL WITHOUT HAVING EVERYTHING FALL APART. IT'S IMPORTANT TO ALWAYS HAVE A VERY CLEAN GRILL TO INHIBIT STICKING. WE ALSO RECOMMEND BUYING A FISH—OR ANY FLEXIBLE— SPATULA. THE ABILITY OF THIS HANDY TOOL TO BEND ALLOWS YOU TO GET UP SNUG AGAINST THE GRILL GRATE AND EASILY LIFT YOUR FOOD RIGHT OFF. THE BEST WAY TO DO THIS IS TO PUSH DOWN WITH THE TIP OF THE SPATULA AT ABOUT A 45-DEGREE ANGLE ON THE GRATE, THEN SLIDE IT UNDER THE FISH. YOU CAN ALSO USE TONGS, TO HELP GUIDE THE PROCESS.

4 (6-oz/170g) striped bass fillets, skin on

2 tbsp/30ml olive oil, for brushing

¼ cup/20g Wet Spice Rub (recipe follows)

2 slices thick-cut bacon

1 small sweet onion, chopped

3 ears corn, shucked (about 1½ cups/225g)

1 cup/150g frozen edamame, shelled and defrosted, or lima beans

½ lemon

1 cup/150g cherry tomatoes, halved

1 tbsp/5g fresh thyme leaves

Equipment: 10"/25cm cast-iron pan, baking sheet fitted with a wire rack, fish spatula, tongs

Prepare the grill for hot two-zone grilling. Pile unlit charcoal on one side of the grill. Fill a chimney with charcoal. Stuff two sheets of newspaper in the bottom of the chimney and light it. When the coals are fully engaged—you should see flames peeking over the top—pour them over the unlit charcoal. Cover the grill and open the vents all the way. If using gas, adjust the temperature on one side of the grill to high.

Brush each fillet on both sides with olive oil. Smear the Wet Spice Rub liberally on the flesh side of each fillet. Set aside and start the succotash.

When the grill temperature reaches 350ºF to 400ºF/177ºC to 204ºC, clean the grill grate. Set a cast-iron pan directly over the fire. Add the bacon and cook until crispy. Remove the bacon from the pan, leaving the fat in the pan, drain on a paper towel and coarsely chop. Place the onion in the pan, cook for 2 minutes directly over the fire, and then move the pan to the cool side of the grill. Add the corn and edamame and cook over the cool side of the grill (you want to just warm the corn and edamame), making sure there is plenty of room close to the fire for the fish.

(continued)

Place the fillets skin-side down around the outside of the fire. Grill for 5 minutes, until the fish is brown and crispy around the edges. Flip the fish and grill for an additional 2 to 3 minutes, until it is just cooked through; it should have an internal temperature of 140°F/60°C. Using tongs and a flexible spatula, carefully remove the fillets and place them skin-side down on a rack set into a baking sheet. Squeeze the lemon over the fish and finish the succotash.

Set the pan back over the fire, stir the succotash and cook for 2 minutes more. Stir in the tomatoes, thyme and chopped bacon and cook for another 2 minutes. Remove from the fire and serve immediately with the fish.

WET SPICE RUB

MAKES ABOUT ¼ CUP/20G

THIS RUB IS BEST IF YOU TOAST AND GRIND THE CUMIN, CORIANDER AND MUSTARD SEEDS YOURSELF, LEAVING EACH A BIT CHUNKY. STORE-BOUGHT GROUND SPICES WORK TOO, BUT BE SURE TO BUY TOP QUALITY.

1 tsp ground cumin
1 tsp ground coriander
1 tsp mustard powder
1 tsp lemon pepper
1 tsp paprika
2 tsp/12g coarse salt
1 tbsp/15ml olive oil

Mix the cumin, coriander, mustard, lemon pepper, paprika and salt in a bowl. Add the olive oil and blend into a paste with a fork. Use immediately or store, covered and refrigerated, for 2 days. Stir well before using.

SMOKY SPICY LAMB CHORIZO

MAKES 10 PATTIES

THIS DIY CHORIZO IS PERFECT WITH EGGS, SALSA AND SOUR CREAM IN THE MORNING, OR IN PITA WITH CUCUMBERS AND YOGURT. WE START OUT SEARING THESE SAUSAGE PATTIES, THEN FINISH BY SMOKING THEM. THIS WILL PROVIDE A KILLER CRUNCH AND BALANCED FLAVOR.

2½ lb/1130g ground lamb

½ cup/40g chili powder

¼ cup/60ml white vinegar

¼ cup/20g minced cilantro

2 jalapeño, serrano or habanero peppers (depending on how hot you like it), cored, seeded and minced

2 tbsp/30ml olive oil

4 cloves garlic, minced

2 tsp/4g red pepper flakes

1 tsp dried oregano

2 tsp/12g kosher salt, plus more, to taste

Freshly cracked black pepper, to taste

Cucumber-Yogurt Sauce, for serving (recipe follows)

Equipment: Apple or cherry wood chunks, or soaked chips

(continued)

Prepare the grill for hot two-zone grilling. Pile the unlit charcoal on one side of the grill. Fill a chimney with charcoal. Stuff two sheets of newspaper in the bottom of the chimney and light it. When the coals are fully engaged—you should see flames peeking over the top—pour them over the unlit charcoal. Cover the grill and open the vents all the way. If using a gas grill, light the gas and adjust the temperature on one side of the grill to high.

In a large mixing bowl, combine all the chorizo ingredients. Season with salt and pepper. Break off a small piece and, in a small sauté pan over medium heat, cook it to taste for salt and pepper levels.

Divide the lamb mixture evenly into 10 balls and flatten each into a ½ inch/13mm-thick patty.

When the temperature reaches 350ºF to 400ºF/177ºC to 204ºC, clean the grill grate. Place the sausage patties on the hot side of the grill and sear for 30 seconds. Rotate 90 degrees and cook for 30 seconds more. At this point they should have dark brown caramelization. Flip and repeat.

Move the sausages to the cool side of the grill, as far away from the fire as possible. Add wood chunks or drained chips to the fire and cover the grill (charcoal only). It will become quite smoky. For gas grills we suggest using soaked chips. Place them in a small disposable aluminum pan with tiny holes poked in the bottom, set it over the hot side of the grill and close the lid. Let smoke for 5 minutes.

Remove the patties from the grill, transfer to a rack and let rest for 3 minutes. Serve with the Cucumber-Yogurt Sauce.

CUCUMBER-YOGURT SAUCE

2 cups/475ml plain yogurt

1 small cucumber, peeled, seeded and minced (about 1 cup/120g)

Juice of 1 lemon (about ¼ cup/60ml)

1 tsp minced fresh mint leaves

1 tsp minced fresh oregano

½ tsp cumin seeds, toasted and ground

Kosher salt and freshly cracked black pepper, to taste

In a medium-size bowl, combine all the ingredients thoroughly. Cover and refrigerate until needed.

OUTDOOR CAST-IRON POTATO GALETTE

MAKES 6 TO 8 SERVINGS

THIS IS A CLASSIC COMFORT FOOD, WHICH PICKS UP A BIT OF SMOKE WHEN PREPARED ON THE GRILL. IT IS TRICKY TO KEEP THE GALETTE FROM STICKING TO THE PAN, SO WE INTRODUCE A TECHNIQUE THAT MAY SEEM A LITTLE FUSSY, BUT IT'S EFFECTIVE. AFTER COOKING THE POTATOES IN A CAST-IRON PAN OVER A MEDIUM FIRE, WE RECOMMEND REMOVING THE PAN AND LETTING THE FIRE TEMPERATURE INCREASE. THEN RETURN THE GALETTE TO THE FLAMES FOR A FEW SECONDS. THE DIRECT HEAT WILL HELP IT RELEASE FROM THE PAN, MAKING SERVING EASIER—AND MAYBE EVEN A LITTLE MORE ATTRACTIVE.

5 large russet potatoes, about 8 oz/230g each, peeled and cut in half

3 tbsp/45ml olive oil

2 tsp/12g kosher salt

2 tsp/5g freshly ground black pepper

2 tbsp/10g fresh thyme leaves

4 cloves garlic, minced

¼ cup/60g butter, at room temperature

Equipment: Mandoline or food processor fitted with slicing blade, 10"/25cm cast-iron pan

Using a mandoline or food processor fitted with a slicing blade, slice the potatoes ⅛ inch/3mm thick. Soak in a large bowl of cold water for 5 minutes. Remove and dry on paper towels. Before proceeding, make sure the potatoes and mixing bowl are completely dry. Return the potatoes to the mixing bowl and toss with the olive oil, salt, pepper, thyme leaves and garlic.

Prepare the grill for hot two-zone grilling. Pile unlit charcoal on one side of the grill. Fill a chimney with charcoal. Stuff two sheets of newspaper in the bottom of the chimney and light it. When the coals are fully engaged—you should see flames peeking over the top—pour them over the unlit charcoal. Cover the grill and open the vents all the way. If using a gas grill, light the gas and adjust the temperature on one side of the grill to high.

Smear the butter inside the cast-iron pan. Spread the potato slices evenly in the pan. To make it fancier, you can arrange them in layers of concentric circles, but the "rustic" look will get them onto your plates faster. Or you can cheat by just arranging the bottom layer in concentric circles, since the galette will be inverted.

When the temperature reaches 350ºF/177ºC, clean the grill grate. Place the pan directly over the fire and cook for 5 to 10 minutes, until the pan is sizzling and the edges of the potatoes just begin to brown. Move the pan to the cooler sider of the grill, cover the grill and cook for 20 minutes.

(continued)

Using high-temperature grilling gloves, remove the pan from the grill. Spray or rub one side of an 18-inch/46cm piece of aluminum foil with cooking oil. Place the foil over the pan, oiled side down. Wearing the mitt, press firmly on top of the foil to compress the potatoes, and crimp the edges of the foil around the pan. Return to the cool side of the grill for 20 minutes, or until the potatoes test soft with a knife poked through the foil. Remove the pan from the grill and leave the lid off, allowing the fire to get hotter.

Remove the foil and place the pan directly over the fire. Wearing gloves to hold the pan in place, use your other hand to work a spatula along the edges of the pan, to loosen the galette. Shake the pan a few times and when the galette appears loose, remove from the grill. Place a platter over the pan and flip. Cool slightly, then slice into wedges and serve.

Cast-iron pan on the grill

GRILLED CORN WITH WHITE MISO BUTTER

FRESH SUMMER CORN HAS LOTS OF NATURAL SUGARS IN IT AND WE LOVE NOTHING MORE THAN COAXING THEM OUT WITH FIRE TO CREATE A BEAUTIFUL CARAMELIZATION THAT'S IMPOSSIBLE TO ACHIEVE ANY OTHER WAY—SORT OF A NATURAL CARAMEL CORN. IT'S IMPORTANT TO KEEP IN MIND THAT WHILE YOU WANT TO ACHIEVE A NICE CHAR, YOU DON'T WANT TO DRY OUT THE KERNELS. DIRECT GRILLING THE EARS THE ENTIRE TIME WILL STEAM AWAY THAT YUMMY CORN JUICE. INSTEAD, WE COOK THEM OVER HIGH HEAT, THEN SLIDE THEM TO THE COOLER SIDE OF THE GRILL, FINISHING THE CORN WITHOUT SUCKING IT DRY.

¼ cup/60g butter, at room temperature

½ cup/120g white (shiro) miso

6 ears corn, shucked

1 tbsp/18g kosher salt, plus extra for serving

3 scallions, cut into thin rings

Place the butter and miso into a mixing bowl and blend thoroughly with a fork. Cover and refrigerate.

Prepare the grill for hot two-zone grilling. Pile unlit charcoal on one side of the grill. Fill a chimney with charcoal. Stuff two sheets of newspaper in the bottom of the chimney and light it. When the coals are fully engaged—you should see flames peeking over the top—pour them over the unlit charcoal. Cover the grill and open the vents all the way. If using a gas grill, light the gas and adjust the temperature on one side of the grill to high.

Remove the miso butter from the refrigerator. When the grill temperature reaches 350ºF to 400ºF/177ºC to 204ºC, clean the grill grate. Grill the corn directly over the fire, turning occasionally, until about one-quarter of the kernels are charred, 3 to 5 minutes. Move the corn to the cooler side of the grill but leave the grill uncovered. Cook until the corn is bright yellow and there are more charred kernels, another 3 to 5 minutes.

Transfer the corn to a serving platter and slather with the miso butter. Sprinkle with the salt, then the scallions. Serve with extra miso butter and salt on the side.

Corn caramelizes directly over the fire.

PEPPER STEAK SKEWERS WITH SUMMER TOMATO SALAD

MAKES 4 SERVINGS

THIS DISH IS REALLY ABOUT SIMPLICITY AND HIGHLIGHTING THE SUMMER AND A GRILL. IT'S A PERFECT APPETIZER. UNLIKE PORK AND CHICKEN SKEWERS, THE GOAL HERE IS TO GET A NICE CRUST WHILE KEEPING THE MEAT RARE, SO WE COOK ON A TWO-ZONE FIRE AT HIGH HEAT. THE HIGH HEAT GIVES YOU THE QUICK CRUST, COOKING QUICKLY KEEPS THE MEAT RARE, AND KEEPING ONE SIDE OF THE GRILL COOL MEANS THE SKEWERS WON'T BURN (AS LONG AS YOU REMEMBER WHICH WAY TO POINT THEM).

10 oz/284g flank steak, fat trimmed (center cut works best)

Freshly ground black pepper

Zest from 1 or 2 lemons

Kosher salt

Olive oil

Summer Tomato Salad, for serving (recipe follows)

10 basil leaves, julienned, for garnish

Equipment: Eight 12"/30cm skewers, soaked in water

Prepare the grill for hot two-zone grilling. Pile the unlit charcoal on one side of the grill. Fill a chimney with charcoal. Stuff two sheets of newspaper in the bottom of the chimney and light it. When the coals are fully engaged—you should see flames peeking over the top—pour them over the unlit charcoal. Cover the grill and open the vents all the way. If using a gas grill, light the gas and adjust the temperature on one side of the grill to high.

Holding a knife at roughly a 70-degree angle, slice the steak against the grain ¼ inch/ 6mm thick by about 1 inch/2.5cm wide.

Lay the slices on a cutting board and cover both sides liberally with black pepper and lemon zest. Gently tap with the back of a spoon to tenderize the pieces and push the lemon and pepper in. Season both sides with salt. Thread the meat onto the skewers, weaving it through 3 or 4 times, depending on the length of the slice. Lightly brush each skewer with olive oil.

When the grill temperature reaches 350ºF to 400ºF/177ºC to 204ºC, clean the grill grate. Place the skewers over the grill with the meat directly over the fire and the exposed wooden ends over the cool side. Grill for 1 minute, then flip and cook for 1 minute more. Remove from the grill and set the skewers on the tomato salad. Garnish with the basil.

SUMMER TOMATO SALAD

4 large heirloom tomatoes, cored, cut into ½"/13mm-thick slices

1 tbsp/15g mustard

1 tbsp/15ml lemon juice

3 tbsp/45ml olive oil

2 tbsp/30ml honey

Kosher salt and freshly cracked pepper, to taste

Arrange the tomatoes in an overlapping pattern on a platter.

In a small bowl, whisk together the mustard, lemon juice, olive oil, honey and salt and pepper. Drizzle the vinaigrette over the tomatoes.

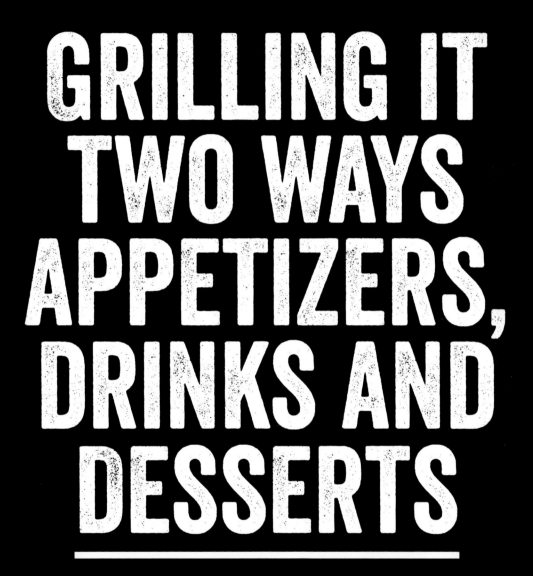

GRILLING IT TWO WAYS APPETIZERS, DRINKS AND DESSERTS

LACQUERED PORK BELLY WITH DIJON AND SOY

MAKES 12 SKEWERS, 4 TO 6 APPETIZER SERVINGS

HERE YOU ARE USING TWO COOKING TECHNIQUES, HOT AND INDIRECT GRILLING. THE FIRST HELPS CARAMELIZE THE MEAT, GIVING IT A NICE CRUNCHY CHEW. THE LATTER WARMS, INTENSIFIES AND CARAMELIZES THE GLAZE.

IN THIS RECIPE WE ASK YOU TO SKEWER STRIPS OF PORK BELLY. THE MEAT IS KIND OF WIGGLY BEFORE IT'S COOKED. FREEZING IT FOR ABOUT 45 MINUTES WILL MAKE IT EASIER TO CUT INTO THE 4" X ¼"/10CM X 6MM STRIPS CALLED FOR HERE.

---

1 cup/240ml water

½ cup/120ml plus 1 tbsp/15ml soy sauce, divided

½ cup/120ml honey or agave nectar

1 jalapeño pepper, stemmed, minced

Juice and minced zest of 1 lime

1 tbsp/5g peeled and minced ginger

¼ cup/60ml Dijon mustard

¼ cup/60ml whole-grain mustard

¼ cup/60ml honey

2 tbsp/10g cilantro leaves

1 tbsp/15ml rice wine vinegar

1 tbsp/12g sugar

1 clove garlic, minced

1 tsp sesame oil

Kosher salt and freshly ground black pepper, to taste

1 lb/450g pork belly, skin removed, cut lengthwise into ¼"/6mm-thick strips (about 4"/10cm long)

Equipment: Twelve 12"/30cm wooden skewers, soaked in water for at least 4 hours. We prefer the thick bamboo type because they hold up to the pork.

Make the marinade: In a small saucepan bring the water, ½ cup/120ml of the soy sauce, honey, jalapeño, lime zest and ginger to a boil over high heat. Remove from the heat, transfer to a bowl and cool to room temperature. Refrigerate, covered, until completely chilled, about 2 hours.

Make the lacquer: In a medium bowl, mix the Dijon and grainy mustards, honey, cilantro, vinegar, sugar, garlic, sesame oil, lime juice and remaining 1 tablespoon/15ml soy sauce and stir until fully incorporated. Season with salt and pepper. Cover and refrigerate until ready to use.

Add the pork slices to the chilled marinade. Cover and refrigerate for at least 4 and up to 24 hours. (If 4 hours, this would be a good time to start soaking the skewers.)

(continued)

Prepare the grill for hot two-zone grilling. Pile unlit charcoal on one side of the grill. Fill a chimney with charcoal. Stuff two sheets of newspaper in the bottom of the chimney and light it. When the coals are fully engaged—you should see flames peeking over the top—pour them over the unlit charcoal. Cover the grill and open the vents all the way. If using a gas grill, light the gas and adjust the temperature on one side of the grill to high.

Remove the pork from brine and skewer each piece.

When the temperature reaches 350ºF to 400ºF/177ºC to 204ºC, clean the grill grate. Place the meat on the hot side of the grill, with the skewer ends on the cold side. Grill for about 30 to 45 seconds, until the meat starts to brown; flip over and repeat. Continue grilling and turning the meat over for about 3 to 5 minutes, until it is golden to dark brown with some charred areas.

When the meat is done, place it on the cool side of the grill, about 3 inches/7.5cm from the hot side. Thickly brush the lacquer on the meat, cover the grill and let set for 2 minutes. Flip the skewers and repeat. Serve immediately, using any leftover lacquer for dipping.

ARNIE PALMER, SORTA

FOR US, DRINKS GO HAND IN HAND, OR AT LEAST IN ONE HAND, WITH GRILLING AND FRIENDS. WE CAME UP WITH THIS RECIPE AS PART OF A QUEST TO MAKE A COCKTAIL THAT CHANGES WHILE YOU DRINK. IT'S NOT A TRADITIONAL ARNOLD PALMER, BUT WE NEVER CLAIMED TO BE TRADITIONAL. IF YOU WANT TO ADD SOME VODKA IT'S CALLED A JOHN DALY, ALSO A GOLFER. HE MAY NOT HAVE BEEN AS GOOD AS ARNOLD, BUT HIS DRINK MIGHT BE BETTER.

THIS RECIPE TAKES A WHILE, BECAUSE YOU NEED TO MAKE ICE CUBES. IT'S FUN AND WORTH THE WAIT.

FOR THE ICED TEA CUBES

2 cups/475ml water

3 black tea bags

Zest of 1 orange

1 star anise

In a small saucepan over high heat, bring the water to a boil. Remove from the heat and add the tea bags, zest and star anise. Remove the tea bags after 2 minutes and let cool to room temperature. Strain the tea and pour into a standard 16-cube ice tray (each square holding about 1 ounce/30ml liquid). Place in the freezer until fully frozen.

FOR THE LEMONADE

1 cup/200g sugar

1 cup/240ml water

1"/2.5cm piece ginger, peeled and smashed with the side of a knife

3½ cups/820ml cold water

½ cup/120ml fresh lime juice (from about 4 limes)

½ cup/120ml fresh lemon juice (from about 2 lemons)

Lemon or lime wedges, for garnish

Mint sprigs, for garnish

In a small saucepan over medium heat, bring the sugar and water to a boil, stirring occasionally, until the sugar dissolves. Remove from the heat and cool to room temperature. Pour into a blender and add the ginger; purée until smooth. Strain through a fine-mesh sieve into a bowl. Stir in the cold water and fresh juices. Refrigerate until ready to serve.

Divide the iced tea cubes among 4 tall glasses and top with enough plain ice cubes to fill the glasses at least halfway; pour the lemonade over them. Garnish with lemon or lime wedges and mint sprigs. If you want to turn your Arnold Palmer into a John Daly, add 1 or 2 ounces/30 or 60ml of vodka to each glass after the lemonade and give a quick stir.

ELVIS'S GRILLED BANANA SPLIT

GRILLING MOST FRUIT IS PRETTY EASY. MANY OF THEM (NOT YOU, BERRIES) ARE FIRM AND EASY TO HANDLE WHEN WARMED OR COOKED ON THE GRILL. BANANAS HAVE A LOT OF NATURAL SUGAR, WHICH MEANS THEY CAN BURN EASILY. AS LONG AS YOU WATCH THEM CAREFULLY, YOU'LL BE OKAY. WE ALSO LIKE TO KEEP THEM IN THE PEEL WHILE COOKING, ESPECIALLY THE RIPE ONES, WHICH MAKES THEM THAT MUCH EASIER TO HANDLE.

¼ cup/60g butter

¼ cup/60g packed brown sugar

¼ cup/60ml really good bourbon (Elvis would want it that way)

¾ cup/195g chunky peanut butter

¼ cup/60g marshmallow fluff

1 tbsp/15ml vegetable oil, for grilling

4 slightly ripe, freckled bananas, skin on, cut in half lengthwise

1 pint/475g vanilla ice cream

½ cup/50 crisped rice cereal

½ cup/120g chocolate chips, preferably mini

Equipment: Grill-safe saucepan

Prepare the grill for hot two-zone grilling. Pile unlit charcoals on one side of the grill. Fill a chimney with charcoal. Stuff two sheets of newspaper in the bottom of the chimney and light it. When the coals are fully engaged—you should see flames peeking over the top—pour them over the unlit charcoal. Cover the grill and open the vents all the way. If using a gas grill, light the gas and adjust the temperature on one side of the grill to high.

When the temperature reaches 350ºF to 400ºF/177ºC to 204ºC, clean the grill grate. Melt the butter in a small saucepan directly over the fire, swirling the pan, until the butter browns and develops a nutty smell. Add the brown sugar, stirring until it is mixed thoroughly. The next step takes a lot of caution because you're playing with fire . . . Very carefully, add the bourbon. Slide the pan to the cool side of the grill and slowly give it a stir. Using a long-handled lighter, carefully light the liquid; you should get a burst of flame. Let the flame burn out, and stir well. Add the peanut butter and fluff, stirring until warm and fully combined. Leave the pan on the cool side of the grill, stirring occasionally, while you grill the bananas.

Brush the oil on the cut sides of the bananas, set them directly over the fire and grill for 2 to 4 minutes, until golden brown. Flip the bananas and grill for 1 minute more, until the skin just begins to separate from the flesh. Transfer the bananas to a plate and let cool for 1 to 2 minutes.

To serve, turn the bananas out of their skins into bowls. Scoop ice cream between the bananas. Drizzle generously with the peanut butter sauce, and garnish with the crisped rice cereal and chocolate chips.

Grill bananas in their skins.

CHAPTER 5

GRILL IT SLOW AND LOW: TWO-ZONE GRILLING

The recipes in this chapter are based on barbecue principles, with the addition of radiant heat. Most barbecue smokers today utilize truly indirect heat. But historically, barbecuing was more nuanced, combining techniques as we do here using basic charcoal (preferred) or gas grills and low, slow, radiant heat. There are lots of ways to cook big cuts of tough meat, and they don't require dedicated or specialized equipment. You will enjoy the payoff in dishes like Slow-Grilled Beef Brisket (page 147), Salt-and-Pepper Picnic Shoulder on Your Kettle Grill (page 150) and Jerk Ribs with Guava Glaze (page 155).

Note: Although you don't need specialized equipment, you do need grill space large enough to accommodate the food in these recipes. Every recipe in this chapter is intended to be cooked on a grill no smaller than 18 inches/45.7cm in diameter.

GRILL-ROASTED WHOLE CHICKEN WITH HONEY AND ROSEMARY

MAKES 2 TO 4 SERVINGS

A PERFECTLY COOKED CHICKEN IS THE STAR OF ANY MEAL, AND THIS IS ONE OF OUR FAVORITES. IT IS IMPORTANT TO TIE THE DRUMS TOGETHER, WHICH WILL HELP WITH EVEN COOKING AND BROWNING. AS WITH MANY OF THE BONE-IN RECIPES IN THIS BOOK, THE TWO-ZONE METHOD HELPS ACHIEVE THE GRILL FLAVOR AND COOK THE BIRD THROUGH WITHOUT BURNING THE SKIN.

4-lb/1.8kg broiler chicken

5 sprigs rosemary, divided

1 lemon, quartered

4 cloves garlic, smashed

2 tbsp/30ml canola oil

1 tbsp/18g kosher salt

1 tbsp/12g turbinado sugar

½ tbsp/3g coarsely ground black pepper

½ tbsp/3g chili powder

¼ cup/60ml warm honey

Equipment: Wire rack set in a baking sheet, butcher's twine (optional)

Stuff the chicken cavity with 4 sprigs of the rosemary, lemon quarters and garlic. Tie the legs with butcher's twine to hold the stuffing inside. Brush the exterior of the chicken with canola oil. Rub the salt, sugar, pepper and chili powder evenly over the entire chicken. Let sit at room temperature while building the fire.

Prepare the grill for low two-zone grilling. Pile unlit charcoal on one side of the grill. Fill a chimney with charcoal. Stuff two sheets of newspaper in the bottom of the chimney and light it. When the coals are fully engaged—you should see flames peeking over the top—pour them over the unlit charcoal. Cover the grill and close the vents 75 percent. If using a gas grill, light the gas and adjust the temperature on one side of the grill to medium.

When the temperature reaches 325ºF/163ºC, clean the grill grate. Place the chicken breast-side up on the cool side of the grill with the legs pointed toward the fire. Cover the grill. Cook the chicken for 1 hour, or until the internal temperature deep in the thigh registers 160ºF/71ºC.

Transfer the chicken to the rack, breast-side down, and let rest for 15 minutes. While the chicken is resting, in a small saucepan over low heat, warm the honey. Remove from the heat and keep warm.

Place the chicken on a cutting board, breast-side up. Discard the stuffing. Carve the chicken into drum, thigh, wing and breast portions. Place on a platter. Snip the remaining rosemary sprig into 5 pieces and sprinkle over the carved chicken. Drizzle with the warm honey and serve.

Ribs are close to but not over fire.

CHARCOAL-GRILLED RIBS: NORTH MEATS SOUTH

THERE'S NOTHING LIKE GRILLED RIBS, BUT FOR MAXIMUM ENJOYMENT, YOU WANT TO MAKE SURE THEY'RE COOKED RIGHT. PERFECTLY GRILLED RIBS SHOULD HAVE A TOOTHSOME, FIRM TEXTURE AND NOT BE FALLING OFF THE BONE. TO TEST FOR DONENESS, HOLD TWO RIB BONES AND PULL IN OPPOSITE DIRECTIONS. IF THE MEAT TEARS EASILY, THE RIBS ARE DONE. IF NOT, PUT THEM BACK ON THE GRILL AND COOK THEM FOR ANOTHER 30 MINUTES. WASH THESE DOWN WITH PEACH MINT JULEPS (PAGE 182).

---

1 rack meaty baby back ribs (also called loin backs), 2½ to 3 lbs/1 to 1.4kg, peeled

1 cup/240ml Vermont Pork Mop (recipe follows)

½ cup/40g Memphis-Style Dry Rub (recipe follows)

Using a paper towel, remove the membrane from the back of the ribs. Rinse the ribs with cold water and place on a sheet pan. Brush the ribs generously on both sides with the Vermont Pork Mop. Refrigerate for up to 1 hour.

Prepare the grill for hot two-zone grilling. Pile the unlit charcoal on one side of the grill. Fill a chimney with charcoal. Stuff two sheets of newspaper in the bottom of the chimney and light it. When the coals are fully engaged—you should see flames peeking over the top—pour them over the unlit charcoal. Cover the grill and open the vents all the way. If using a gas grill, adjust the temperature on one side of the grill to high.

When the temperature reaches 350ºF/177ºC, clean the grill grate. Remove the ribs from the refrigerator and re-baste with any mop that has accumulated on the sheet pan. Sprinkle the ribs all over with 2 tbsp/10g of the Memphis-Style Dry Rub and place them as close to the fire as possible without being right over the charcoal. Cover the grill and cook for 1 hour, adjusting the vents and adding charcoal as needed to maintain a consistent 350º/177ºC temperature. After 1 hour, test the ribs for doneness.

Remove the ribs from the grill and sprinkle generously with the remaining 6 tablespoons/30g dry rub. Slice and serve.

VERMONT PORK MOP

½ cup/120ml cider vinegar

½ cup/120ml maple syrup

¼ cup/60ml water

¼ cup/60ml ketchup

2 tbsp/30ml barbecue dry rub (your choice, but we recommend Memphis-Style; recipe follows)

1 tsp chipotle powder or cayenne pepper

In a medium bowl, mix all the ingredients well. Keep at room temperature while cooking or cover and refrigerate for up to 2 weeks.

MEMPHIS-STYLE DRY RUB

¼ cup/20g paprika

2 tbsp/10g garlic powder

1 tbsp/5g onion powder

2 tbsp/30g kosher salt

1 tbsp/2g dried thyme

1 tbsp/5g MSG

½ tbsp/3g ground coriander

½ tbsp/3g ground cumin

½ tsp curry powder

In a medium bowl, combine all the ingredients well. Store in an airtight container for up to 2 weeks.

SLOW-GRILLED BEEF BRISKET

MAKES 10 SERVINGS

WE OFFER A LOT OF ADVICE IN THIS BOOK ABOUT THE FINER DETAILS OF DIFFERENT GRILLING METHODS. BUT FROM DIRECT GRILLING TO GRILL-ROASTING TO LOW TWO-ZONE COOKING, ONE OF THE MOST IMPORTANT TASKS FOR GRILLING MEAT, IN PARTICULAR, TO PERFECTION DOESN'T ACTUALLY TAKE PLACE ON THE GRILL. WE CANNOT STRESS ENOUGH THE IMPORTANCE OF RESTING MEAT BEFORE SERVING IT. IF YOU CUT INTO OR SERVE IT RIGHT AWAY, THE JUICE WILL NOT HAVE TIME TO REDISTRIBUTE AND WILL DRAIN FROM THE MEAT, LEAVING YOU WITH A DRY MEAL. WE SUGGEST RESTING SMALLER PIECES OF MEAT FOR 5 TO 10 MINUTES AND LARGER PIECES FOR 15 TO 30 MINUTES.

5- to 7-lb/2.3- to 3.2kg beef brisket flat, with fat

¼ cup/60ml yellow mustard

3 tbsp/54g kosher salt

1 tbsp/5g freshly cracked white pepper

1 head roasted garlic, processed into a paste

½ cup/120ml red wine

½ cup/120ml low-sodium beef broth

½ tbsp/3g fresh oregano

½ tbsp/3g fresh thyme

8 cherry tomatoes

½ fennel bulb, cored and thinly sliced

½ sweet onion, thinly sliced

1 carrot, sliced

Equipment: Drip pan, roasting or aluminum pan, heavy-duty aluminum foil, probe thermometer

Brush the brisket with the mustard, then sprinkle evenly with the salt and pepper. Place on a baking sheet and refrigerate.

Prepare the grill for low two-zone grilling. Pile unlit charcoal on one side of the grill. Fill a chimney with charcoal. Stuff two sheets of newspaper in the bottom of the chimney and light it. When the coals are fully engaged—you should see flames peeking over the top—pour them over the unlit charcoal. Cover the grill and close the vents 75 percent. If you are using a gas grill, light the gas and adjust the temperature on one side of the grill to medium.

When the temperature reaches 300ºF/149ºC, clean the grill grate. Place the brisket on the cool side of the grill, fat-side up. Position a drip pan below the brisket. Cover the grill and cook for 3 hours, or until a thermometer inserted into the meat reaches 170ºF/77ºC. Rotate the brisket after 1 hour to develop an evenly caramelized crust. Add more charcoal and adjust the vents as necessary to maintain the fire temperature.

While the brisket is cooking, prepare the braising liquid. In a blender on high speed, mix together the garlic, wine, broth, oregano and thyme. Pour into a bowl and set aside until ready to use.

In the bottom of a roasting or aluminum pan that is large enough to hold the brisket and also fits on the grill, layer the tomatoes, fennel, onion and carrot.

(continued)

Brisket after 3 hours.

Fat-side down, on top of vegetables.

Resting brisket.

Slice brisket against the grain.

Cut in ¼-inch/6mm-thick slices.

Fan slices to serve.

After 3 hours, place the brisket, fat-side down, on top of the vegetables. Pour the braising liquid over the brisket and cover the pan tightly with heavy-duty aluminum foil. Return the covered brisket to the grill and cook for about 2 hours more, until a thermometer registers 195ºF/91ºC.

Remove the pan from the grill and rest the brisket. Place the brisket fat-side up in a 9"x 13"/23 x 33cm baking dish. Process the braising liquid and vegetables briefly in a blender or press them through a fine sieve. Pour the liquid over the brisket, tent with foil and let sit at room temperature for 1 hour. Slice the brisket against the grain in ¼-inch/6mm-thick slices. Fan the slices on a platter and drizzle with some of the braising liquid.

SALT-AND-PEPPER PICNIC SHOULDER ON YOUR KETTLE GRILL

MAKES 8 TO 10 SERVINGS

THIS IS NOT BARBECUE PORK FOR THE PURISTS. IF YOU WANT THAT, AND WE OFTEN DO, CHECK OUT OUR RECIPES IN *WICKED GOOD BARBECUE*. THAT STUFF IS SERIOUS BARBECUE. BUT THAT DOESN'T MEAN YOU SHOULDN'T MAKE THIS RECIPE. THIS WILL BLOW YOUR MIND WITH ITS SIMPLE METHOD AND COMPLEX FLAVORS AND TEXTURE. THE GOAL HERE IS TO GET THE OUTSIDE CRUNCHY LIKE CHICHARRONES AND THE INSIDE NICE AND JUICY. IT WILL TAKE SOME PATIENCE—AND PROBABLY A BEER OR TWO. YOU WILL BE GRILLING THIS FOR A WHILE. AND TRY NOT TO PEEK. LIFTING THE LID TO LOOK IN WILL ONLY MAKE THE TEMPERATURE FLUCTUATE, WHICH WILL EXTEND THE COOKING TIME.

6- to 9-lb/2.7- to 4kg pork picnic shoulder

½ cup/120ml vegetable oil

½ cup/144g kosher salt

¼ cup/20g coarsely ground black pepper

Basic Vinegar Sauce (recipe follows)

Equipment: Probe thermometer, 2 aluminum pans approximately 10"/25cm wide

Rinse the shoulder under cold water and dry well with a paper towel. Score the skin around the shank portion by cutting a criss-cross pattern with a sharp knife. With your hands, rub the vegetable oil into the meat. Mix the salt and pepper in a plastic cup and sprinkle evenly all over the exterior of the shoulder. Place the shoulder onto a baking sheet and refrigerate while preparing the grill. Don't forget to wash your hands.

Prepare the grill for low two-zone grilling. Pile unlit charcoal on one side of the grill. Fill a chimney with charcoal. Stuff two sheets of newspaper in the bottom of the chimney and light it. When the coals are fully engaged—you should see flames peeking over the top—pour them over the unlit charcoal. Cover the grill and close the vents 75 percent. Remove the top grill grate and place the aluminum pan on the side without charcoal to catch the drippings. If using a gas grill, light the gas and adjust the temperature on one side of the grill to medium. You don't need a drip pan with a gas grill.

(continued)

Remove the pork shoulder from the refrigerator (and grab a cold beer).

When the grill temperature reaches 300°F/149°C, clean the grill grate. Place the shoulder on the grate above the drip pan, fat-side up. Close the lid and, for charcoal, position the exhaust vent above the shoulder. Close the bottom vents and the top vent about halfway. Every 45 minutes or so, add a large handful of charcoal to the second aluminum pan and sprinkle it over the fire. A lot of kettle grills have a hinged grate that makes it easy to add charcoal to the fire. If yours doesn't, you will have to pick up the whole grate with the shoulder on it, nudge it to the side and add charcoal on the fire. Not all charcoal is created equal. Some is very dense and will burn longer, while others are lighter and burn quickly, so you'll have to adjust the charcoal-feeding schedule based on how quickly the fire burns.

If you like a soft bark, after 5 hours, wrap the shoulder in aluminum foil. This will also decrease the cooking time. If you prefer a crustier bark and you have plenty of beer left, skip the foil. Cook until the internal temperature of the meat registers 195°F/91°C, approximately 6 to 8 hours total.

Transfer the shoulder to a cutting board and tent with foil. Rest the shoulder at room temperature for 1 hour. Serve with cold beer and Basic Vinegar Sauce.

BASIC VINEGAR SAUCE

MAKES 3 CUPS/700ML

3 cups/700ml cider vinegar

½ cup/120g light brown sugar

2 tbsp/30ml hot sauce, such as Crystal or Tabasco

2 tsp/10g kosher salt

2 tsp/10g black pepper

1 tsp red pepper flakes

In a medium saucepan over medium heat, bring all the ingredients to a simmer, whisking until fully incorporated. Remove from the heat and cool completely. Transfer to a container and refrigerate, covered, for up to 1 month.

CHARCOAL SELECTION

Okay, so you carefully selected that beautiful piece of protein and are gearing up to cook one of our sometimes-challenging-yet-always-worth-it recipes. Don't settle for mediocrity now by picking up a bag of average charcoal at the hardware store. Instead, your admirable pursuit of excellence should most definitely extend to charcoal selection. While we almost always prefer hardwood charcoal, we concede that there are rare times when briquettes are acceptable. And you may find those times even more frequent than rare. Here are some pros and cons of both:

BRIQUETTES

→ They are inexpensive and widely available.

→ Many brands contain non-wood fillers. Seek out brands labeled "natural" that use only vegetable starch as a binder.

→ They generate significant ash. Grills that are not designed to allow for ash buildup, such as ceramic grills, don't work well with briquettes.

→ Every bag contains briquettes with the same uniform size and density. You can fit more charcoal briquettes in the grill than hardwood, because the pieces fit together more tightly, which results in longer burn times. This makes it a good choice for longer cooking two-zone recipes.

→ Extruded coconut charcoal is an environmentally friendly, hot-burning charcoal often used in yakitori grills. The only downside is it's difficult to find in the U.S.

LUMP (HARDWOOD)

→ Look for brands that highlight manufacture from specific woods, like maple or apple.

→ For the most part, avoid brands made with kiln-dried wood floor scrap, which is lightweight and flavorless. In a pinch it is okay for quick, hot fires because it lights easily.

→ Each bag of lump charcoal contains different sizes, shapes and density. We embrace variability, relying more on sensory cues to find that right cooking temperature. With experience, you will, too.

→ See Resources (page 184) for our favorite types of lump charcoal. If you can swing the space, buy a pallet of the good stuff in the spring before grilling season rolls into full gear. You'll be happy to have it on hand.

JERK RIBS WITH GUAVA GLAZE AND GRILLED BANANAS

WE LOVE THE INTENSE HEAT AND FLAVOR OF THE HABANERO. IF YOU'RE NOT A FAN OF THE HEAT, TRY ADDING A SMALL AMOUNT OF THE PEPPER UNTIL YOU HAVE OBTAINED YOUR COMFORT LEVEL. OR JUST TRUST US AND GO FOR IT.

OUR GOAL FOR THIS RECIPE IS TO GET THE RUB TO "CRUST UP" WHILE COOKING, WHICH GIVES THE RIBS A FABULOUS, DYNAMIC FLAVOR. TRADITIONALLY, PIMENTO WOOD IS USED TO COOK JERK-STYLE FOOD IN JAMAICA. ANY KIND OF HARDWOOD (WE PREFER CHUNKS) WILL WORK WELL TO ROAST THESE RIBS. KEEPING THEM IN THE SAME SPOT ON THE GRILL HELPS, TOO.

---

4 habanero peppers, stems removed, minced

¼ cup/60g brown sugar

4 tsp/7g ground cinnamon

2 tsp/4g cumin seeds, toasted and ground

2 tsp/4g dried thyme

2 tsp/4g dried oregano

2 tsp/4g ground allspice

1 tsp ground nutmeg

2 tbsp/36g plus 2 tsp/12g kosher salt

4 tsp/7g ground black pepper

¼ cup/60ml white vinegar

¼ cup/60ml canola oil

2 racks baby back ribs, about 2 lb/900g each, peeled

Grilled Bananas (recipe follows)

Guava Glaze, for serving (recipe follows)

Make the rub: In a small bowl, mix together the habanero, brown sugar, cinnamon, cumin, thyme, oregano, allspice, nutmeg, salt, pepper, vinegar and oil. Set aside.

Place the racks of ribs on a large baking sheet and coat completely with the rub. Refrigerate for 24 hours. Every 6 to 8 hours, reapply the rub that has dripped off, then flip the racks over.

Prepare the grill for hot two-zone grilling. Pile the unlit charcoal, preferably pimento wood (see Resources, page 184), on one side of the grill. Fill a chimney with charcoal. Stuff two sheets of newspaper in the bottom of the chimney and light it. When the coals are fully engaged—you should see flames peeking over the top—pour them over the unlit charcoal. Cover the grill and open the vents all the way. If using a gas grill, light the gas and adjust the temperature on one side to high.

When the temperature reaches 350°F/177°C, clean the grill grate. Place the two racks meat-side up as far as possible from the hot side of the grill. Cover the grill and roast the ribs for 30 minutes. Flip and rotate each rack, so the one that was closest to the fire is now the farthest, and both are meat-side down. At this point you might have to throw a little more charcoal on the fire to maintain the heat. Grill the ribs for 30 more minutes, then flip and rotate again, adding a small amount of coal. Continue to cook, covered, for 30 minutes more. The meat should be browning at this point.

(continued)

After 1½ hours the ribs should be close to done. A thermometer inserted into the meat should register 170ºF/77ºC and the meat should be tender. (Note to our barbecue friends: This is not barbecue-tender style. It's a grill-roast.)

Remove the ribs and let cool on a wire rack. Carefully spread the coals and let them cool to a low fire (you should be able to hold your hands over the fire for no more than 8 to 10 seconds) for grilling the bananas.

When ready to serve, on a large cutting board, cut the ribs between the bones. Arrange the ribs and bananas on a large platter in an alternating pattern. Drizzle the Guava Glaze over all. Don't forget the napkins.

GRILLED BANANAS

IT'S SUPER IMPORTANT TO MAKE SURE YOU CLEAN THE GRILL BETWEEN COOKING THE RIBS AND THE BANANAS. THIS TROPICAL FRUIT HAS A TENDENCY TO STICK, WHAT WITH THE HIGH SUGAR CONTENT AND ALL.

3 ripe bananas, cut in half lengthwise, skin on

Vegetable oil, for grilling

Lightly rub the cut side of the bananas with oil.

When you can hold your hands over the grill for 8 to 10 seconds, grill the bananas, cut-side down, for 2 to 3 minutes, until they are slightly brown. Flip over and grill-roast for 1 minute more. Transfer to a platter.

GUAVA GLAZE

MAKES ABOUT 2½ CUPS/590 ML

1 cup/240g diced guava paste

½ cup/120ml white vinegar

½ cup/120ml water

½ cup/120ml pineapple juice or orange juice

1 tbsp/5g minced fresh ginger

1 tsp curry powder

½ tsp dried thyme

1 tsp kosher salt

In a small heavy saucepan, cook all the ingredients over low heat, stirring, until they are fully blended, 10 to 15 minutes. The paste will take a little while to soften and blend in but once it does you will have a rich, dynamic sauce for your killer ribs.

LEMON AND FRESH HERB GRILL-ROASTED LEG OF LAMB

MAKES 4 TO 6 SERVINGS

FOR THIS RECIPE WE USE WHAT WE CALL A DOUBLE-BANK METHOD, WHICH IS PERFECT FOR LARGE ROASTS BECAUSE IT ALLOWS YOU TO CARAMELIZE THE MEAT ON ALL SIDES EVEN THOUGH YOU ARE ROASTING IT OVER INDIRECT HEAT. WE RECOMMEND USING TWO REMOTE THERMOMETERS, SETTING ONE PROBE NEAR THE MEAT (SEE THE POTATO METHOD, PAGE 102) AND ONE IN IT. THIS ALLOWS YOU TO MONITOR THE TEMPERATURES OF THE COOKING SURFACE AND THE FOOD. WE ALSO LOVE TO ADD HARDWOOD CHUNKS DURING THE COOKING PROCESS. WITH THE LONG COOKING TIME, YOU'LL GET WONDERFUL SMOKE FLAVOR.

Leaves from 1 sprig rosemary

6 sage leaves

1 cup/80g curly parsley

3 cloves garlic, roughly chopped

Zest of 1 lemon

1½ tsp/7.5g Dijon mustard

3 tbsp/15g freshly ground fennel seeds

⅔ cup/160ml vegetable oil

Boneless leg of lamb (about 4 lb/ 1.8kg)

Kosher salt and freshly cracked black pepper, to taste

1 tbsp/5g minced fresh mint leaves

¼ lemon

Olive oil, for serving

Equipment: Aluminum drip pan, 2 remote thermometers, butcher's twine

In the bowl of a food processor fitted with a steel blade, combine the rosemary, sage, parsley, garlic, lemon zest, mustard, fennel and vegetable oil and pulse to create a paste. Add a bit more oil if the mixture clumps up or is too thick.

Place the lamb on a baking sheet and trim any large pieces of gristle or sinew, leaving most of the fat in place. Smear both sides with the herb mixture. Cover and refrigerate overnight.

Remove the lamb from the refrigerator and prepare the grill for double-bank two-zone grilling. Fill a charcoal chimney with lump charcoal but do not light. Pile half the unlit charcoal to the right and the other half to the left. Set an aluminum drip pan between the charcoal piles and fill halfway with water. Refill the charcoal chimney, stuff newspaper in the bottom of the chimney and light it. When the coals are fully engaged—you should see flames peeking over the top—pour them over the unlit charcoal. Cover the grill and open the vents all the way. If using a gas grill, light the gas and turn on the front and rear, or outside burners, to high.

While the grill is heating, re-truss the lamb. Sprinkle both sides with salt and pepper. Roll the lamb back into a roast-like shape, fat side out, and truss with butcher's twine (see page 161).

(continued)

When the temperature reaches 350ºF to 400ºF/177ºC to 204ºC, clean the grill grate. Place the lamb on the grill directly above the drip pan and cover the grill. For gas grills, place the lamb over the unlit burner. Grill-roast for 45 minutes, or until the internal temperature registers 120ºF/49ºC for rare (our preference) or 130ºF/54ºC for medium. If necessary, add a couple of small pieces of charcoal to each pile while the lamb is roasting to keep a consistent temperature.

Remove the lamb from the grill and place on a cutting board to rest for 20 minutes. Using kitchen shears, snip away the butcher's twine. With a carving knife, thinly slice the lamb. Sprinkle with the mint, squeeze on the lemon juice and drizzle with a thin line of olive oil.

Boneless leg of lamb.

Trim any large pieces of gristle or sinew.

Herb wet rub.

Rub with herb mixture.

Smear both sides.

Double-bank two-zone grilling set up.

Roll the lamb.

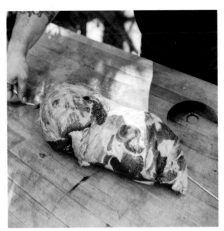
Flip cut side down.

Place on long strand of butcher's twine.

Wrap twine around each end.

Create a loop around the leg.

Pull twine through the loop.

Tighten.

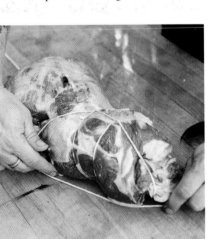
Repeat.

Pull tight on each loop.

Create 5 or 6 ties.

Tie off excess twine.

Cut excess.

Ready for the grill.

Lamb cooks directly over drip pan.

PERFECT HOLIDAY TURKEY ON YOUR GRILL WITH TURKEY BACK GRAVY, CORNBREAD DRESSING, BASIC BRINE AND GRILLED APPLES

MAKES 10 TO 12 SERVINGS

IN HER 1989 BOOK *THE WAY TO COOK*, JULIA CHILD TOOK A NEW APPROACH TO ROASTING TURKEY, TAKING THE BIRD APART BEFORE—RATHER THAN AFTER—COOKING. HER REASONING, ALWAYS SOUND, WAS THAT COOKING WHOLE TURKEYS ALWAYS TAKES FOREVER AND THE DIFFERENT PARTS COOK AT DIFFERENT RATES. JULIA SUGGESTED DECONSTRUCTING THE TURKEY, ROASTING THE PARTS SEPARATELY, THEN REUNITING THEM IN THE ROASTING PAN TO FINISH UP ALL TOGETHER. IT WORKS.

WE DON'T KNOW WHETHER JULIA EVER TRIED GRILLING HER THANKSGIVING TURKEY, BUT—NO SURPRISE—WE DO IT ALL THE TIME. AND WE'VE ENCOUNTERED THE SAME ISSUES OUTSIDE THAT WE USED TO RUN INTO INSIDE. SO WE TRIED TAKING THE TURKEY APART AND GUESS WHAT! PERFECT, JUICY TURKEY! WE DON'T REASSEMBLE THE TURKEY ON THE GRILL. WE SAVE THAT FOR WHEN WE BRING IT BACK INDOORS.

---

1 gallon/3.8L Basic Brine (recipe follows)

12- to 14-lb/5.4- to 6.4kg turkey

Kosher salt and freshly ground black pepper, to taste

½ cup/120ml low-sodium chicken broth

½ cup/120ml barbecue sauce

¼ cup/60ml apple cider vinegar

Grilled Turkey Back Gravy (recipe follows)

Cornbread Dressing (recipe follows)

2 tbsp/30ml vegetable oil

1 tbsp/5g freshly ground black pepper

(continued)

HOLIDAY GRILLING SCHEDULE AT A GLANCE

DAY 1

→ Make brine

→ Grill legs

→ Grill back and neck

→ Make stock for gravy

DAY 2

→ Make gravy

→ Grill breast

→ Rewarm legs

→ Make dressing

→ Grill apples

1½ tsp/3g chili powder

½ cup/120ml maple syrup

Grilled Apples (recipe follows)

Fresh sage, for garnish

Equipment: 2-gallon/7.6L brining bag, baking pan lined with a cooling rack, two 18"/46cm squares heavy-duty foil

Day 1: Make the brine and deconstruct the turkey (see photos, pages 166-167). Remove and discard any trussing and pop-up thermometer. Refrigerate the neck, back and wings for Grilled Turkey Back Gravy.

Place the leg quarters on a baking sheet and season both sides with salt and pepper.

Place the turkey breast, meat-side down, into the brining bag and pour in the cold brine. Refrigerate for 12 to 24 hours.

Grill the legs. Prepare the grill for two-zone grilling. Pile unlit charcoal on one side of the grill. Fill a chimney with charcoal. Stuff two sheets of newspaper in the bottom of the chimney and light it. When the coals are fully engaged—you should see flames peeking over the top—pour them over the unlit charcoal. Cover the grill and close the vents 75 percent. If using a gas grill, light the gas and turn just one side on to medium.

When the temperature reaches 300ºF/149ºC, clean the grill grate and place the leg quarters skin-side down on the cool side of the grill for about 1 hour, or until the internal temperature of the leg reaches 160ºF/70ºC.

(continued)

Place turkey breast-side down on a cutting board.

Remove neck, giblets bag.

Create a line on each side of the backbone.

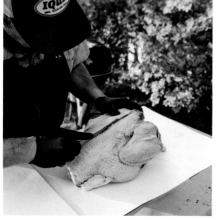

Cut along one side of backbone.

Cut along other side.

Begin to pull back out of cavity.

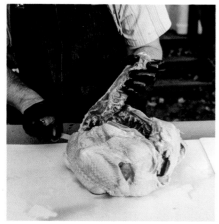

Pull up on back.

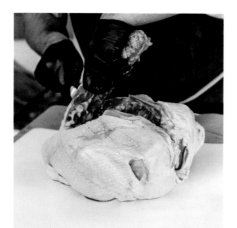

Continue cutting.

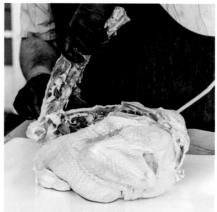

Remove back.

Cut between knuckle of wing and tip.

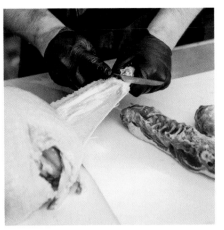

Remove wing tip.

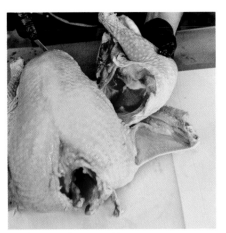

Cut between breast and leg.

Remove leg and trim fat.

Repeat and remove other leg.

Trim rib bones.

Breast lays flat and is ready to go.

Trimmed breast and legs.

Fully deconstructed turkey.

If making the gravy, position the back and neck closer to the fire for 30 to 45 minutes, until slightly charred.

In a small saucepan over medium heat, combine the chicken broth, barbecue sauce and apple cider vinegar until warm. Transfer each leg to an 18 inch/46cm piece of heavy-duty aluminum foil and baste both sides generously with the broth mixture. Tightly wrap the legs in foil and return to the cool side of the grill for another 30 minutes, or until a thermometer inserted into the thick part of a leg registers 180ºF/82ºC. Remove from the grill, unwrap the foil and let cool to room temperature. Reseal the foil, place the legs on a baking sheet and refrigerate overnight.

Meanwhile, use the browned turkey back and neck to make the turkey stock for the Grilled Turkey Back Gravy. Cool, and refrigerate the stock, covered.

If making the cornbread dressing, place the cornbread and white bread cubes on a baking sheet and leave out, uncovered, overnight.

Day 2: Cook the breast and rewarm the legs. Remove the breast from the brine and place on a baking sheet lined with a cooling rack. Pat dry with paper towels and return to the refrigerator for at least 1 hour and up to 6 hours.

While the breast is drying in the refrigerator, finish the stock and make the gravy.

Prepare the grill for two-zone cooking (see above). When the temperature reaches 300ºF/149ºC, brush the breast with the oil and sprinkle with the black pepper and chili powder. Place the breast on the cool side of the grill with the thicker wing end pointed toward the fire. Grill for 1 hour.

Remove the legs from the refrigerator and add them, still sealed in foil, to the cool side of the grill. Check the internal temperature of the turkey breast. Continue cooking until a thermometer inserted into the deepest part of the breast (near the wing joint) reads 155ºF/68ºC, approximately 1 more hour. Tent the turkey with foil if the skin becomes too dark.

Remove the breast and the legs from the grill, and place the breast on a clean baking sheet. In a small saucepan, warm the maple syrup over medium heat and spoon it over the breast. Tent loosely with foil and let rest for 45 minutes while you bake the stuffing and grill the apples.

To serve, fill the center of a large platter with the Cornbread Dressing. Set the breast on the dressing. Place a leg quarter, with drum pointed inward, on each side of the breast. Decorate the platter with the Grilled Apples and sage leaves. Pass the Grilled Turkey Back Gravy on the side.

BASIC BRINE

1 gallon/3.8L water, divided

¾ cup/60g kosher salt

¾ cup/150g sugar

¼ cup/60ml maple syrup

10 sage leaves

1 head garlic, cut in half horizontally

10 whole black peppercorns

In a large pot over high heat, bring 2 quarts/1.9L of the water to a boil. Remove from the heat and add the salt, sugar, maple syrup, sage leaves, garlic and peppercorns, stirring until the salt dissolves. Pour into a large bowl, stir in the remaining 2 quarts/1.9L of cold water and refrigerate for at least 6 hours or overnight.

GRILLED TURKEY BACK GRAVY

THIS IS A TWO-DAY RECIPE.

3-lb/1.4kg turkey or chicken wings

1 turkey back

1 turkey neck

Reserved trimmings from deconstructed turkey

1 onion, sliced

2 stalks celery, chopped

1 carrot, chopped

1 gallon/3.8L cold water

½ cup/40g parsley, sprigs and stems

Kosher salt and freshly ground black pepper, to taste

¼ cup/60g butter

½ cup/60g flour

1 tbsp/15ml apple cider vinegar

1 tbsp/5 sage, cut into chiffonade

Place the wings, turkey back and neck, turkey trimmings, onion, celery and carrot in a deep, 8-quart/7.6L stockpot. Cover with the cold water. Bring to a boil over medium-high heat, then reduce the heat to a simmer. Skim any foam off the top, add the parsley and simmer slowly, without stirring, for 4 to 6 hours. Strain the broth through a fine-mesh sieve or cheesecloth. Cool in a low-sided wide pan or bowl at room temperature, whisking occasionally to release the steam, for 1 hour. Refrigerate overnight.

Remove the broth from the refrigerator and scrape the fat from the surface, reserving 2 tablespoons/30ml. Bring the broth to a boil, skimming off any bits that rise to the top. Lower the heat and simmer the broth until it is reduced to about 5 cups/1.2L, about 15 minutes. Season well with salt and pepper.

In a medium saucepan over medium-low heat, melt the butter and reserved turkey fat. Add the flour and whisk constantly for 5 minutes, until lightly colored. Carefully add 1 cup/240ml of the hot broth, whisking until smooth. Slowly add the remaining 4 cups/960ml broth, whisking constantly. Return to a simmer and cook, stirring occasionally, until thickened, about 10 minutes. Add the vinegar and sage and keep warm, ideally in a double boiler, until ready to serve.

CORNBREAD DRESSING

2 tbsp /30g butter, softened, for pan

1 onion, sliced

1 cup/120g sliced celery (2 large stalks)

1 cup/70g sliced button mushrooms (about 4 oz/113g)

2 tbsp/30ml olive oil

2 tbsp/10g chopped sage

1 tsp kosher salt

¾ tsp freshly ground black pepper

One 9" x 13"/23 x 33cm loaf day-old, unsweetened cornbread, cut into 1"/2.5cm cubes (about 8 cups/960g)

3 large slices day-old crusty white bread, cut into 1"/2.5cm cubes (about 2 cups/100g)

1½ cups/355ml chicken stock or broth

Equipment: Grill-safe baking pan

Coat the inside of a 9" x 13"/23 x 33cm baking pan with the softened butter; set aside.

Preheat the oven to 350ºF/170ºC/gas mark 4 or, while the turkey is resting, raise the grill temperature to 350ºF/170ºC by opening the vents and adding half a chimney of lit charcoal.

In a large sauté pan over medium heat, sauté the onion, celery and mushrooms in the olive oil until soft, about 15 minutes. Remove from the heat and stir in the sage, salt and pepper.

In a large bowl, combine the cornbread, white bread, sautéed vegetables and broth until just incorporated. Spoon into the prepared baking dish. When the grill temperature reaches 350ºF/170ºC, place the dressing on the cool side of the grill, cover the grill and bake for 30 minutes, or bake in the oven for 30 minutes. Mound the dressing on serving platter.

GRILLED APPLES

6 crisp apples, such as Gala, Fuji or Honeycrisp, cored and cut into quarters

2 tbsp/30ml vegetable oil, for brushing

1 tbsp/5g chili powder

2 tbsp/30ml agave nectar, at room temperature

1 tbsp/5g mint leaves, cut into chiffonade

When the cornbread stuffing is done, brush the apples with the oil and sprinkle with chili powder, then grill on all sides for 15 to 20 minutes. Arrange around the turkey, drizzle with the agave nectar and top with the mint

PUMPKIN BREAD IN A CAN WITH CHOCOLATE SEA SALT BUTTER

USING THE GRILL AS AN OVEN, AS IN THIS RECIPE, IS DIFFICULT BECAUSE ONE OF THE TRICKIEST ASPECTS OF COOKING OVER CHARCOAL IS LEARNING HOW TO MONITOR THE TEMPERATURE OF THE FIRE. BUT THE HINT OF SMOKE THE CHARCOAL IMPARTS GIVES WHATEVER YOU ARE BAKING A UNIQUE FLAVOR YOU AND YOUR GUESTS WON'T SOON FORGET. TO SOME EXTENT, THIS TYPE OF GRILLING COMES WITH EXPERIENCE. AFTER DOING IT AGAIN AND AGAIN (AND AGAIN), YOU GET A FEEL FOR THE FIRE. BUT SOMETIMES IT IS IMPORTANT TO KNOW THE EXACT TEMPERATURE OF THE GRILL. MANY EXPERIENCED GRILLERS RELY ON THE TEMPERATURE GAUGE ON THE GRILL COVER. THE MORE SERIOUS AMONG US USE A REMOTE THERMOMETER WHERE THE RECEIVER, WITH TEMPERATURE INFORMATION, IS IN ONE LOCATION AND A PROBE IS DANGLED INTO THE GRILL THROUGH A COVER VENT TO MEASURE THE TEMPERATURE OF THE GRILL ENVIRONMENT. THERE ARE A VARIETY OF THESE GAUGES, WHICH WE ADDRESS IN THE TOOLS SECTION (SEE PAGE 10).

---

5 tbsp/65g sugar, divided, plus more for dusting

1 cup/120g flour

¾ tsp baking powder

½ tsp kosher salt

½ tsp ground ginger

½ tsp cinnamon

¼ tsp baking soda

⅛ tsp nutmeg

4 tbsp/60g butter, softened

¾ cup/185g pumpkin purée

1 egg

3 tbsp/45g sour cream

½ tsp vanilla extract

Chocolate Sea Salt Butter, for serving (recipe follows)

Equipment: 3 small (10¾-oz/318ml) soup cans, washed well and dried; 6"/15cm wooden skewer

Prepare the grill for hot two-zone grilling. Pile unlit charcoal on one side of the grill. Fill a chimney with charcoal. Stuff two sheets of newspaper in the bottom of the chimney and light it. When the coals are fully engaged—you should see flames peeking over the top—pour them over the unlit charcoal. Cover the grill and open all the vents. If using a gas grill, adjust the temperature on one side of the grill to high.

Spray the insides of the soup cans with cooking oil spray. Pour about 1 tablespoon/15g sugar into one can and slowly rotate to coat the whole inside. Tip any remaining sugar into the second can and repeat, then do the same with the third can, so all cans are fully coated.

In a medium-size mixing bowl, sift together the flour, baking powder, salt, ginger, cinnamon, baking soda and nutmeg. Set aside.

(continued)

In the large bowl of an electric mixer, cream together the butter and remaining 4 tablespoons/50g sugar until fluffy, about 3 minutes, scraping down the sides of the bowl. Add the pumpkin purée and continue beating until fully incorporated. Add the egg, beating to blend. Add the sour cream and vanilla, and beat on medium speed until well blended.

Add the dry ingredients in 3 batches, scraping down the sides each time, and mix on low until well blended. Divide the batter evenly among the soup cans, filling each about half full.

When the grill temperature reaches 350ºF/170ºC, clean the grill grate. Set the cans upright on the cool side of the grill and cover the grill. Bake, shifting the position of the cans for even heating every 10 minutes, until the breads are golden brown and a wooden skewer inserted into the center comes out clean, about 30 minutes.

Wearing heatproof gloves, transfer the cans to a wire rack and let cool for 10 minutes. Pop the breads out onto the rack. Slice them and serve immediately with Chocolate Sea Salt Butter. You can also place the slices on a baking sheet lined with parchment paper, spread the Chocolate Sea Salt Butter on each slice and set the sheet in a covered grill for about a minute, until the butter is melted.

CHOCOLATE SEA SALT BUTTER

MAKES ½ CUP/120G

½ cup/120g butter, softened

3 tbsp/23g confectioner's sugar

2 tbsp/16g unsweetened cocoa powder

1 tbsp/15ml your favorite bourbon or rye

1 tsp large flake sea salt, such as Maldon

In the bowl of a stand mixer fitted with the paddle attachment, mix the butter, sugar, cocoa powder and bourbon on medium speed until fully incorporated, scraping down the sides. Add the salt and mix for 15 seconds on low speed. Transfer to a serving bowl and refrigerate, covered, until needed. Let stand at room temperature until soft before using.

You can also roll the butter into a log in parchment paper, cover it well with plastic wrap and refrigerate.

GRILL IT
SLOW AND LOW
APPETIZERS
AND DRINKS

SICHUAN CHICKEN LOLLIPOPS WITH CUMIN-FLAVORED DRY SPICE

MAKES 8 LOLLIPOPS, 4 APPETIZER SERVINGS

THESE ARE MEATY AND BIG FLAVORED, PERFECT FOR A BACKYARD BARBECUE, WHERE YOU'LL HAVE CHICKEN IN ONE HAND AND A BEER IN THE OTHER. HERE WE DRAW INSPIRATION FROM CHINA'S SICHUAN PROVINCE, WHERE FLAVORS IN MANY WAYS ARE SIMILAR TO WHAT WE LIKE ABOUT AMERICAN BARBECUE. THEY HAVE A WONDERFUL BALANCE OF BOLD, SPICY, TANGY AND SWEET, AND PAIR BEAUTIFULLY WITH COLD BEER.

ONE WAY WE LIKE TO ACHIEVE A PUNCH OF FLAVOR IS TO INTRODUCE A SPICE RUB AT THE END OF THE COOKING PROCESS, AS OPPOSED TO THE MORE TYPICAL APPLICATION AT THE BEGINNING. A FINISHING RUB CREATES A BRIGHT, INTENSE, SPICY FINISH. IT'S WORTH THE EFFORT TO FIND SICHUAN PEPPERCORNS; YOUR GUESTS' TONGUES WILL BE TINGLING HAPPILY FOR DAYS.

8 chicken legs

½ cup/120ml honey

2 tbsp/30ml soy sauce, preferably low-sodium

2 tbsp/30ml hoisin sauce

Juice of 1 tangerine

1 tsp ground ginger

2 tbsp/36g kosher salt

2 tbsp/10g Sichuan peppercorns (or white peppercorns)

2 tbsp/10g cumin seeds, toasted

½ tbsp/3g Chinese five-spice powder

Prepare the chicken legs. Using kitchen shears, cut off the knob at the end of the bone. Using a chef's knife, scrape the meat down the bone from the knuckle end, pushing it toward the meaty end to create a "lollipop." Remove the tendons using a pair of tweezers or pliers. Wrap the now bare bone with foil.

In a small bowl, mix the honey, soy sauce, hoisin, tangerine juice and ginger. Place the chicken in a large plastic zipper bag and pour in the mixture. Remove all air from the bag, seal it and refrigerate for 1 to 2 hours.

In another small bowl, combine the salt, peppercorns, cumin and five-spice powder. Using a spice grinder, process into a fine powder, working in batches if necessary. Store in a plastic cup or a measuring cup with a spout.

(continued)

Prepare the grill for low two-zone grilling. Pile unlit charcoal on one side of the grill. Fill a chimney with charcoal. Stuff two pieces of newspaper in the bottom of the chimney and light it. When the coals are fully engaged—you should see flames peeking over the top—pour them over the unlit charcoal. Cover the grill and close the vents 75 percent. If using a gas grill, light the gas and adjust the temperature on one side of the grill to medium.

When the temperature reaches 325ºF/163ºC, clean the grill grate. Remove the chicken from the refrigerator. Take the lollipops out of the bag and place them directly on the grill grate very close to, but not directly over, the fire, with the bones pointing up. Discard any remaining honey-soy mixture.

Cover the grill and cook the chicken, rotating every 15 minutes, for 1 hour, or until a meat thermometer inserted into the thickest part of a lollipop reads 165ºF/74ºC. If the chicken starts to burn, move it to the cooler side of the grill. Remove the lollipops from the grill and place on a platter. Dust completely with the dry rub. Remove the foil and serve.

GALLON OF BLOODY MARY

MAKES 1 GALLON/3.8L, ABOUT 12 SERVINGS

TOO OFTEN WE ARE SERVED BLOOD MARYS THAT ARE WATERY AND LACK FLAVOR. WE AVOID THAT PROBLEM BY MIXING OURS THE DAY BEFORE, WITHOUT ICE. AS THE DRINK SITS OVERNIGHT, THE FLAVORS WILL BLOOM. RIGHT BEFORE SERVING, WE POUR OVER ICE. IT'S A GREAT WAY TO START A DAY OF GRILLING.

1 bottle (750ml) top-shelf vodka

½ cup/120g prepared horseradish

¼ cup/60ml Worcestershire sauce

Juice of 1 lemon

2 tbsp/30ml chipotle hot sauce

1½ tbsp/8g ground black pepper

2 (46-oz/1.4L) cans tomato juice

½ cup/40g your favorite barbecue dry rub

¼ lemon wedge

1 recipe Sweet, Spicy, Smoky Grilled Shrimp Cocktail (page 53) or 12 lemon wedges, for garnish

Equipment: Clean, empty 1-gallon/3.8L jug with lid

Combine the vodka, horseradish, Worcestershire, lemon juice, hot sauce and pepper in an empty plastic 1-gallon/3.8L jug with a lid. Cover and shake well. Add the tomato juice almost to fill (there should be about 1 inch/2.5cm of space at the top of the jug). Shake well and refrigerate for at least 1 hour and preferably overnight. It will keep for up to 5 days in the refrigerator.

To serve, rim a pint glass. Spread the barbecue dry rub in a small, flat dish or saucer. Moisten the rim of the glass with the lemon wedge, and invert the glass into the rub, twisting a bit for good coverage.

Fill the glass halfway with ice. Give the Bloody Mary jug a good shake and pour over the ice. Garnish with a grilled shrimp or a wedge of lemon.

PEACH MINT JULEPS

MAKES 4 SERVINGS

THIS DRINK SCREAMS SUMMERTIME TO US. A FEW OF THESE, AND WE'RE NOT GRILLING ANYTHING; SO MAYBE THIS SHOULD BE THE DESSERT.

YOU SHOULD BE ABLE TO FIND PEACH PURÉE IN THE FROZEN SECTION OF YOUR MARKET OR ONLINE. CANNED PURÉED PEACHES ARE A GOOD ALTERNATIVE. IF YOU GO FOR THIS OPTION, YOU CAN USE THE SYRUP IN THE CAN INSTEAD OF MAKING YOUR OWN SIMPLE SYRUP.

½ cup/100g sugar

½ cup/120ml water

20 mint leaves, divided, plus 4 sprigs for garnish

1 cup/240g peach purée (see Resources, page 184)

10 oz/284ml bourbon (we like Bulleit)

In a small saucepan over medium heat, bring the sugar and water to a boil, stirring occasionally, until the sugar is dissolved. Remove from the heat and add 10 of the mint leaves. Cool to room temperature. With a slotted spoon, remove the mint leaves and add the remaining 10 leaves. Let stand for at least 10 minutes.

Strain the minted simple syrup into a 1-quart/940ml pitcher. Stir in the peach purée and bourbon, and pour over 4 ice-filled glasses. Garnish with the mint sprigs and drink up.

RESOURCES

GRILLS

CHARCOAL

Our gold standards: http://weber.com/grills/series/one-touch/one-touch-gold-2675, http://weber.com/grills/series/performer

Premium model: www.cajungrill.com/cajungrill.html

Budget model: www.americanagrills.com

CERAMIC

http://primogrill.com

www.biggreenegg.com

GAS

Must have two burners, ideally three for two-zone cooking.

Our favorite: http://weber.com/grills/series/genesis

Premium model: www.vikingrange.com

Budget model: www.brinkmann.net/products/details.aspx?item=810-8411-5

CHIMNEYS

http://store.weber.com/accessories/category/cook/tools/1349

CLEANING EQUIPMENT

http://store.weber.com/accessories/category/clean/1455

www.earthstoneinternational.com/cleaning/grill-stone

CHARCOAL

www.wickedgoodcharcoal.com

www.basquescharcoal.com/products.php

www.pimentowood.com

GLOVES AND MITTS

Ansell Neox® neoprene: www.grainger.com/product/ANSELL-Chemical-Resistant-Glove-2AF71

www.firecraft.com/product/charcoal-companion-flame-resistant-grill-mitt/bbq-gloves-bbq-mitts

THERMOMETERS

www.thermoworks.com/products/thermapen

Premium model: www.thermoworks.com/products/alarm/chefalarm.html

Budget model: www.taylorusa.com/classic-digital-oven-thermometer.html

MISCELLANEOUS

Hickory smoke powder: www.spicebarn.com

Sichuan peppercorns: www.thespicehouse.com

Frozen peach purée: www.gourmetfoodworld.com, www.markys.com

ACKNOWLEDGMENTS

We would like to thank …

Our testers, in particular Nancy Boyce. It is impossible to overstate how much you do for us. Also, Lorri Allen, Dave Frary, Eric Frase, Don Geiger, Lori McKeon, Lisa Melnick, George Pelz, Mike Rosenthal, Chris Sargent, Gail Gurney Smith, Kevin J. Smith and Marc Stitt.

John Delpha, Andrea Falcione and John "The Commish" Phillips, Eric Pyenson and Nick Stellino for recipe development.

Brendan Burek for recipe development and support.

Wilson Diaz Hernandez for recipe production. Melissa Cawley for recipe support.

Joe Yonan for recipe contributions from *The Fearless Chef*.

Will Kiester for believing in us again, and the rest of the team at Page Street.

Sorel Denholtz for divine inspiration.

Ken Goodman . . . you did it again.

Andy would like to thank Molly Dwyer and Tyler Firth for holding down the fort at 647, Ms. Sarah Blodgett and the entire 647 team, and the beautiful Ms. Rice Wales.

Chris would like to thank Jenny, Ethan and Jaimie, the most important eaters in my life; Norm "Pop-Pop" Hart, world's best storyteller and hotcake cook; and Andy and Andrea—if it were easy, everyone would do it.

Andrea would like to thank Eric, Craig and Luke, who make my life delicious.

ABOUT THE AUTHORS

Andy Husbands, the award-winning chef/owner of Tremont 647, has been enticing patrons with his adventurous American cuisine at the South End (Boston) neighborhood restaurant and bar for well more than a decade. A James Beard "Best Chef" semi-finalist, Husbands competed in the sixth season of Fox television network's *Hell's Kitchen* with Gordon Ramsay. When he's not in the kitchen or working with his favorite charities, Husbands is on the barbecue trail with his award-winning team, iQUE. His first cookbook, *The Fearless Chef*, is currently in its second printing. He is also the author, with Chris Hart and Andrea Pyenson, of *Wicked Good Barbecue* and *Wicked Good Burgers*.

Chris Hart is the 2009 winner of the Jack Daniels Invitational World Championship Barbecue competition and has dominated the barbecue circuit for the past 10 years with his team iQUE. In 2010, Chris cooked an elaborate barbecue tasting menu at the James Beard House in New York City. The following year he was a contestant on Food Network's first season of *Best in Smoke*. This is his third cookbook with Andy and Andrea.

Andrea Pyenson has been writing about food and travel for more than a decade. Her work has appeared in various publications, including the *Boston Globe, Edible Boston, Edible Cape Cod, Washington Post, Fine Cooking*, msn.com and oneforthetable.com. This is her third cookbook with Andy and Chris.

INDEX

"THIS BOOK WAS WRITTEN FOR THOSE AMONGST US WHO WANT TO MASTER THE ART OF GRILLING."

—NICK STELLINO, CELEBRITY CHEF

"ANDY AND CHRIS'S RECIPES ARE 100% CROWD PLEASERS."

—JAMIE BISSONETTE, CHEF/CO-OWNER OF COPPA AND TORO IN BOSTON, AND TORO NYC

"THIS BOOK IS A TERRIFIC RESOURCE FOR ANYONE WHO WANTS TO LEARN HOW TO GRILL LIKE A MASTER."

—JOANNE CHANG, CHEF/OWNER OF FLOUR BAKERY AND MYERS + CHANG IN BOSTON AND AUTHOR OF THE BESTSELLING COOKBOOK, *FLOUR*

"ANDY AND CHRIS HAVE MADE THE MYSTERIOUS ART OF GRILLING EASY AND APPROACHABLE. I ESPECIALLY LIKE THE WAY THEY LOWER THE HEAT AND USE THE GRILL TO LAYER COMPLEX SMOKY FLAVORS IN THEIR FOOD."

—GORDON HAMERSLEY, AUTHOR OF THE BESTSELLING, *BISTRO COOKING AT HOME* AND CHEF/CO-OWNER OF HAMERSLEY'S BISTRO IN BOSTON

"I'M SO STOKED ON THIS BOOK! ANDY AND CHRIS JUST HELPED ME TAKE MY GRILLING SKILLS TO THE NEXT LEVEL! IT'S PARTY TIME!"

—JOE "THE KID" SIROIS, MIGHTY MIGHTY BOSSTONES

"TO ALL THE GREAT COOKS AND EATERS IN OUR LIVES. YOU KNOW WHO YOU ARE."

PAGE STREET
PUBLISHING CO.

First published in 2014 by
Page Street Publishing Co.
27 Congress Street, Suite 103
Salem, MA 01970
www.pagestreetpublishing.com

Distributed by Macmillan; sales in Canada by The Canadian Manda Group; distribution in Canada by The Jaguar Book Group.

17   16   15   14   1   2   3   4   5

ISBN-13: 978-1-62414-042-6
ISBN-10: 1-62414-042-4

Library of Congress Control Number: 2013958196

Cover and book design by Page Street Publishing Co.
Photography by Ken Goodman

Printed and bound in the U.S.A

Page Street is proud to be a member of 1% for the Planet. Members donate one percent of their sales to one or more of the over 1,500 environmental and sustainability charities across the globe who participate in this program.